IT'S **NOT** A PLOT TO DRIVE YOU CRAZY!

IT'S **NOT** A PLOT TO DRIVE YOU CRAZY!

A toolbox of practical parenting skills for everyday use

Fran Kammermayer

This book is dedicated with love to Jerry, Sophie, Mike, and Nick.

National Library of Canada Cataloguing in Publication Data

Kammermayer, Fran, 1952-
It's not a plot to drive you crazy!: a toolbox of practical parenting skills for everyday use/Fran Kammermayer; Cheryl Andrews, editor; Jim Fee, illustrations.

ISBN 0-9731764-0-7

1. Parenting. 2. Child rearing. I. Andrews, Cheryl. II. Title.

HQ769.K35 2002   649'.1   C2002-911141-2

Editing: Cheryl Andrews
Illustrations: Jim Fee Illustration
Design: Blakeley Design

Contents

Part 3: Tools for Talking and Listening

Part 4: Tools for Disciplining With Love

Acknowledgments

Writing this book has been a labour of love, which was brought to fruition by some special people whom I would like to acknowledge and thank:

My husband, Jerry, who always believed I could share my experiences in a book and encouraged me to do so. His love and support helped to make this book a reality.

My wonderful children, Sophie, Mike, and Nick, who taught me so much about being a parent. They urged me to keep going with this book, allowed me to share their stories in it, and tolerated their preoccupied mother with patience and love.

My editor, Cheryl Andrews, who devoted herself wholeheartedly to this project, and many times went beyond the call of duty. Her enthusiasm, dedication, and stars carried me through some of the more difficult times in the writing process. She taught me to think like a writer, and I could not have gone through this process without her.

My friend, Judith Walker, also a proficient editor, who came to my rescue on more than one occasion. She spent many long hours with me "playing" with words to make sure I really said what I meant.

My illustrator, Jim Fee, who provided touches of humour during the long hours I spent at the computer.

My book designer, Gary Blakeley, who patiently explained the concepts of design to me, reassuring me often with the words, "Don't worry about that, Fran, I'll take care of it."

My heartfelt thanks go to you all.

My thanks also go to all the parents, teachers, and caregivers who have worked with me and shared their experiences. I wish them all the best as they journey on with the children in their lives.

Introduction

"Why don't you just move in with us, Fran?" is a request many parents jokingly make during the last session of one of the parenting courses I teach.

Parents often think they need an expert, someone outside of the family, someone who's been there before, to solve their daily parenting challenges. But they don't. They already have the important resources of love, common sense, and gut instinct to guide them. It's always reassuring to know that parenting experts can help with the more difficult parenting issues, but parents can also add to the knowledge they already have by assembling their own toolbox of practical skills. This "toolbox" will help them parent with confidence through many of the typical everyday situations.

With a counselling skills diploma and several years of experience as a preschool teacher, I began to facilitate parenting courses in 1991 for a family services agency. While raising my own three children, I continued to work with parents as a parent educator, and in 1999 I became a Certified Canadian Family Educator and Parenting Consultant. Over the past ten years, while facilitating parenting courses, workshops, and presentations, I have gained invaluable information about parenting from the thousands of parents who have shared their experiences with me. Together we have listened, shared, laughed, and groaned as we talked about the everyday situations that busy parents face. Their numerous questions and stories often provided some reassurance that many of us faced similar challenges during the sometimes overwhelming responsibility of parenting. It was those parents who inspired this book.

In listening to the many common concerns of these parents, I saw the need for an easy-to-use resource book that parents can turn to in the midst of fast-paced lives. Since you can't have a parenting consultant on call, it will help to have your own toolbox of useful skills to assist in your everyday parenting. Life at home is likely to be more harmonious when we have skills at our fingertips that work for children of all ages. So this book presents practical, down-to-earth tips and examples that will make your job as a parent easier and more enjoyable.

This book is also about our children and their journey towards independence. As parents described the obstacles and frustrations they faced, I encouraged them to try to imagine what the situations were like from the child's point of view. With that new understanding we were able to develop appropriate strategies that respected the needs of parents and children. I've included some of those strategies in this book as well.

Often, after making a presentation on a parenting topic, I face a lineup of parents who want to ask me "just one quick question" about their child. The difficulty is that there are seldom any quick-fix solutions for parenting challenges. Effective, consistent parenting takes time and planning, having the right tools at hand, and knowing when to use them.

Many parents have told me that sometimes they felt as if their children were trying to drive them crazy. That's where the title of this book comes from. It is not our children's mission to test our sanity, although we may sometimes feel that's what they're trying to do. They are on a journey towards adulthood and they rely on us to set clear limits and guide them as they explore their world. When we have a selection of parenting skills to choose from, we can more easily help them to achieve their goals of independence, responsibility, and happiness. If we can parent with consistency, respect, and understanding, we may reduce some of the challenges and be able to enjoy our children's daily discoveries with them.

This book is divided into four parts. Part 1 describes the tools that help establish respectful parent and child relationships. Part 2 provides tools for the daily challenges that crop up at home and in public. Part 3 deals with issues that call for communication skills and Part 4 considers the differences between discipline and punishment, and ways to help children become more responsible and accountable for their actions. A concise toolbox skill summarizes each topic. Some of these skills you'll be able to use right away, and some can be tucked into your toolbox for use in the future.

It's never too soon, or too late, to start a parenting toolbox – no matter what the ages of your children, no matter what their stage of development. I hope that having a toolbox full of useful skills will make your parenting easier and bring you more pleasure.

PART 1

Basic Parenting Tools

1 The Toolbox

Toolbox Skill

Plan your approach to parenting. Gather useful skills for your toolbox.

Like many of the life skills we acquire, parenting is made easier with the right tools. Yet most of us become parents, anticipating that we can do the job with little or no training. We think we will know what to do because we were, after all, once children ourselves. But every child is unique, and even when we have experienced some parenting with our first child, the second and subsequent children seldom follow the same behaviour patterns as the first.

When I had my first child, I thought I knew all about parenting. After all, I had some counselling skills and had taught preschool for several years. I had a lot to learn. Having my own children was not the same as looking after other people's children. I found that by sharing my experiences with other parents and listening to their challenges, I gained very valuable information. Reading parenting books written by experts also provided useful insight, and I gradually began to recognize the importance of forming a parenting plan, setting goals, and having the right tools for the job.

Now in my work as a parent educator I am asked many of the same questions. "How do I handle tantrums?" "My child is telling lies. What do I do?" "I can't take the rudeness. How should I respond?" "I just want to know how to get my child to listen to me." Often, I sense that these parents have the solutions themselves, but just need encouragement and a few tools for the situation. A toolbox of skills seemed to be the answer, to give parents the confidence to take the helm and to navigate the voyage with their children.

Tools that are used daily include setting limits, being consistent, using choices, and modelling respectful communication. Then there will be occasions when a parent needs the tools of creativity or encouragement to gently nudge a child towards trying something new. The tools of using flexibility in certain situations, or writing special notes to children may be only needed for occasional use. As our children grow older, we may require the tool of applying appropriate consequences to help them become responsible.

By sharing other parents' stories as well as my own in this book, I hope parents will be encouraged to fill their own toolbox with new ideas and skills. When you have the right tools, parenting can be joyful, rewarding, and fun. As you select and use appropriate parenting tools from your toolbox, your relationships with your children can strengthen and grow.

Parents receive no salary, but the rewards are still priceless. What could be more wonderful at the end of a day than a hug from your child, accompanied by the words, "I love you best in the whole, wide world!" Those moments are more precious than gold.

2 Parenting with Confidence

I believe parents have more internal resources for good parenting than they often realize. They may sense what would be the right way to handle a situation, but they also need the appropriate tools and a concrete plan of action. Acquiring some knowledge about children's typical developmental stages may help parents to gain more confidence in their parenting skills. There are some parenting challenges that do require the advice of an expert. But there are also many times when parents just need to follow their instincts, combined with using some practical tools. Perhaps the following story will explain what I mean.

One Saturday, Tara and her father went to the bank. There was a small play area for children where Tara, an active, eighteen month old, loved to play while her Dad took care of business. So far, Tara had been an easygoing child. Her parents had adjusted to having a little one around, despite lack of sleep and a complete change of lifestyle. Until now, they had enjoyed each of Tara's new stages and were confident with their parenting prowess.

Dad finished his banking and, turning to Tara, said, "Let's go home now, Tara." To his astonishment, Tara replied, "No! Go away, Daddy." Dad was quite taken aback. This defiance was a new phenomenon. He tried to coax her into leaving, but Tara was adamant. She wanted to stay. Other customers were now watching the interaction with amusement, which added to Dad's growing discomfort. Finally, not knowing what else to do, he picked up his daughter and carried her kicking and screaming out of the bank.

After this incident, Tara's defiance manifested itself in all sorts of different ways. Her favourite word became "No." Daily battles raged, as she entered what many label the "terrible two" stage. It is at this time that a child discovers her own voice and self-determination. This stage is an important step towards independence, and it is normal, rather than "terrible." Her parents were unsure of how best to respond to Tara's new and defiant behaviour. They felt they needed some expert advice. This was when I met them, and heard the question so often asked by parents of toddlers: "What happened? Our child has always been so easy to manage, but now she won't do anything we want her to."

When I asked Tara's parents if they thought that she was behaving normally for her age, they told me that she probably was. They were right. They can trust their instincts. If these parents talked with other parents of toddlers, they would likely find that all of them have experienced similar challenges. It is now very important that Tara's parents set firm limits and show consistency in their responses to her. By doing so, they will help Tara to realize which of her behaviours are acceptable and which are not, as she continues with her journey of self-discovery. If her parents are inconsistent with her, she may be confused and behave inappropriately.

Tara's Dad followed his gut instinct to remove her from the bank. Had he given in to Tara's demands to stay, she would have learned that making a fuss gets you what you want. If Dad had given some advance warning about leaving, it might have reduced Tara's resistance. He could have helped her to finish her play by spending a few moments with her. If she still refused to leave, Dad might have had to carry Tara out, but at least he would have been respectful and aware of her needs.

There are lots of valuable resources available to parents such as parenting books, courses, and information on the Internet. With so much advice to choose from, parents must still use their own common sense to know what advice will best suit them and their child. Common sense and gut instinct are both vital components of good parenting. By combining their own instincts with useful advice from parenting experts, parents will gain more confidence in their parenting role.

3

Ignoring Your Inner Voice

The true experts on children are their parents. No one knows a child quite like a parent does. Most of the time, parents are expert at knowing what is best for their child. There are occasions, though, when, despite knowing what is best, we ignore our inner voice because of external circumstances.

Toolbox Skill

Be guided by your inner voice, and have the right parenting tools at hand.

The fully loaded plane left Toronto for England at 10:30 pm. I didn't relish the idea of spending seven hours trying to sleep sitting up, but I didn't feel so sorry for myself when I noticed the young family sitting across the aisle from me. Dad and a five-month-old baby occupied two seats, while Mom and a three-year-old boy sat behind them. Having made overnight flights with my own children before, my heart went out to these parents. The little boy's name was Trevor, and Mom did a great job of keeping him amused with games and stories, while Dad fed the baby and then held her while she slept. After a while, Mom suggested that Trevor try to sleep. She knew her small son was tired, and that he needed his rest.

By now Trevor was overtired, and intent on annoying both parents with constant demands to sit first with his Dad and then back with his Mom. I could sense that both parents' patience was wearing thin. At midnight, a meal was served. This acted as a distraction, but Trevor was only interested in the dessert, a rather rich slice of chocolate cake. His Mom suggested that he should eat something more nutritious first, but Trevor wasn't having any of that nonsense. It was either to be cake, or a scene!

His parents quickly discussed the possible results of eating such rich cake on an empty stomach. Both knew it wasn't wise, but Mom, ignoring her inner voice, capitulated with "You can only have the cake, Trevor, if you promise to go to sleep right after you've finished." To have that cake, Trevor would have agreed to anything. He wolfed down his cake, followed by his mother's piece as well. The next few hours were not happy ones as Trevor, now fuelled by sugar, continued his constant demands for attention, first from one parent, then the other. I heard his poor, exhausted parents say, "Perhaps that cake wasn't a good idea." Eventually, to his parents' great relief, Trevor did doze off, but woke about an hour later and threw up. His mother looked at me as we scrambled for plastic bags and napkins, and said sheepishly, "I should have known better." Just as the plane began its final descent, Trevor finally fell sound asleep.

Even experts make mistakes that go against their better judgment. I think we can all understand why these poor, tired parents deviated from doing what was right for their son and allowed him to eat such rich cake. Arguing with Trevor about the cake may have resulted in a tantrum, and they were in a confined space, surrounded by people trying to sleep. Had they been at home, I'm sure Trevor would have been offered choices other than cake, and it wouldn't have mattered if he were unhappy or had a tantrum. It might have helped if Mom had brought her own supply of food for Trevor and refused the airline meal, eliminating the temptation of the cake. Alternatively, she might have been able to distract him with a new toy or book, while quietly removing the offending cake. Mom and Dad could have taken turns sitting with the baby, while the other sat with Trevor. Especially for those times when we are exhausted, it helps to have the right tools to handle the situation.

4

The Changing Role of Parenting

Toolbox Skill

Taking a parenting course can provide enlightenment, support, and reassurance to parents.

"My seven year old son is running the household," admitted one mother to the other members of a parenting group. "He refuses to cooperate, won't listen, and tells us everything we ask of him is dumb. He's only seven but he has the attitude of a teenager. I'm tired of the incessant arguing. I have to nag about everything. Every day when we come in from school, he drops his coat on the floor. I ask him at least five times to hang it up. Then I get mad, or I hang it up myself. Why can't he just do what we ask the first time?"

This mother was very confused about her role as a parent. She had two PhDs and a very busy career life, but tried hard to make lots of time for her son. She told me her home life seemed out of control, and she needed some help to gain new confidence with her parenting. Many of the parents I work with share the same frustration that this mother was experiencing.

Some of the uncertainty about parenting today is very understandable. In the past ten to fifteen years, life has changed dramatically for many parents. No longer is it the norm for one parent to stay home. Many parents are balancing full time jobs and parenting as well. Lifestyles are frenetic and time is in short supply. This doesn't mean these busy people can't be good parents, but they seem very unsure about their parenting skills.

When I talk to parents and listen to their concerns, I realize many of them are unaware of the normal developmental phases of children, in spite of the wealth of parenting information available. These parents have less time to focus on their parenting and fewer opportunities to chat with other parents with children of similar ages. It can be so reassuring to discover that another parent is also having difficulty with a three year old who won't brush his teeth, or that other ten year olds leave their homework to the last minute, too. What a relief to know that your teen is not the only fifteen year old who refuses to be seen in public with a parent. The added bonus of chatting with other parents is that sometimes they have found ways to overcome some of the common difficulties and are usually more than happy to share their experiences. "It's such a relief to know that I'm not alone" is a comment frequently written on evaluation forms at the end of each of my parenting courses.

At the end of the parenting course, the mother with the two PhDs gave me a hug of thanks. The classes had provided her with the information she needed to understand her son's behaviours, and also gave her a new set of parenting skills. She learned to ask her son what he had to do once they arrived home. He was expected to hang up his coat before anything else. Noticing and encouraging her son's efforts to please, no matter how small, resulted in more cooperation. She discovered the benefits of being consistent, and began using logical consequences for her son that taught him responsibility. In addition, by listening to other parents' concerns and challenges, she realized that she was not alone. The support from the group renewed her confidence and encouraged her to keep going. We met again some months later, and she was now a more relaxed parent who was finding new enjoyment in guiding her son on his life's journey.

5 The Journey

From the moment they are born, children are on a journey. I use the analogy in my parenting classes of children travelling through a long tunnel. The tunnel has firm, but flexible, rubber sides, and a golden glow at the far end. Children are drawn to this golden glow like a moth attracted to a flame. They must reach the glow because it promises fulfillment. As they journey through the tunnel, they frequently bounce off the sides, then return to the centre and continue on their way. Parents quickly grasp the concept that they are the rubber sides, helping the children to stay on course, and that the golden glow is the independence of adulthood. Parents help children to reach their maturity by providing guidance, limits, and stability.

Toolbox Skill

Parenthood is a journey for both parent and child. Learning about yourself as you parent will help you to parent with compassion. Growing up never ends.

As children journey towards adulthood, they make hundreds of discoveries about the world around them and how they fit in. "Who am I, and where do I belong?" is what they most want to know. They will need to experiment and find out what works and what doesn't. The testing of limits will be tiresome at times for parents. A little one having tantrums, an older child forgetting to give you important notices from school, a teen who stays out later than agreed, will all take their toll on parents. Of course there will be lots of successes, too. The first words from a toddler, a performance in a school play, or passing the driving test, will be some of the many causes for celebration.

Parents will also find themselves on a journey. As parents encounter each new phase of their child's development, they will make new discoveries about themselves. Before I became a parent, I considered myself to be calm, patient, and easygoing. Children changed all that. Being a parent led me to discover many of my shortcomings. All of a sudden, I had to master my impatience and lack of tolerance. Giving unconditional love to my children was not always an easy task. Parents are definitely candidates for sainthood and deserve recognition for their efforts. The journey is often like an obstacle course but well worth the trip. As their children grow up, parents may find they "grow up," too.

6 Being a Best Friend

Toolbox Skill

Act like a parent, not a best friend.

I would be lost without my best friends. They are the people I can share my innermost self with. Some of my very best friends know me better than I do. My best friends are good listeners, they don't give advice, and they trust me to solve my own problems. Best friends support us through the good times and the bad.

In our role as parents, we wear many different hats each day: chauffeur, nurse, administrator, confidante, and advisor, to name a few. One hat we must avoid wearing is the "best friend" hat. Sometimes parents look quite shocked when I tell them not to be best friends with their children. It needs some explanation.

Parents have some similarities to best friends. We know our children better than anyone else. We listen to them, and are available when they need us. But there the similarities end. A big part of our job as parents is to set limits, and best friends do not set limits for each other. Of course we will be friendly with our children, and they will see us as their friends, but the role of best friend is only appropriate once the child reaches adulthood. Children need the adults in their lives to guide them and keep them safe. As children go through childhood, they are relying on parents, relatives, and teachers to model the best ways to cope with life's challenges.

Once metamorphosis takes place and the child emerges as a fully responsible, contributing adult member of society, then a best friend relationship is possible.

7 Setting Limits

Toolbox Skill

An important part of a parent's role is to set limits. Limits guide your child safely towards independence.

Setting limits requires firm resolve on the part of parents. If parents are too concerned about upsetting their child, they will find setting limits very difficult. Outwardly children may not appear to like limits, but inwardly they feel a lot more secure when they know the rules. Limits will need to be altered as children grow older, and parents have to make the decisions on how far each limit can be extended. A parent will make all the decisions about a suitable bedtime for a four year old. A nine year old will want to participate in setting the time for bed, and may be allowed to stay up longer on weekends and holidays. A teenager will want to stretch parental limits regarding curfew times to the ultimate degree.

How much independence can we allow our children? This is another difficult issue for parents. There is a fine line between allowing children to move towards independence, and keeping them safe. Letting go of parental control is tricky business. It would be so much easier if we could just control everything. However, if we never let go, our children would not reach independence and would live with us forever.

When our daughter, Sophie, was fourteen years old, she informed us that she was now able to take care of herself, and should be allowed to stay out until 2 am. Naturally, we told her that this suggestion was totally unacceptable to us. Her response was that, since she had proved to us on numerous occasions how sensible she was, we should now allow her the freedom to choose the time she came home at night. We explained that our job was to guide her and to set limits so that she could become truly independent.

My wise husband then came up with a foolproof description of independence. He explained to our daughter that true independence requires physical stability, emotional stability, and financial stability. She believed she had the first two requirements, but acknowledged that she was still dependent on us financially. Reluctantly, Sophie agreed to abide by our rules about curfews.

8 The Influence of Our Parents

Toolbox Skill

Reflect on and discuss the ways you and your partner were parented. The knowledge will help you to develop a solid parenting plan for your own children.

A parent will often say to me, "I can't believe it. I sometimes hear myself sounding just like my parents. I hear words coming out of my mouth that I vowed I would never, ever say to my children!" Parents are often amazed when such expressions surface, and are relieved when other parents admit they have similar experiences. Statements made to children like "You're driving me crazy," or "You'll be the death of me," seem to bubble up from a hidden place inside us. They can be messages we received from our own parents, and are often the first words that come out in stressful times. Usually these comments lie dormant until triggered by either a high level of frustration or fatigue.

The parenting we have received influences our own parenting. When we examine the way we were parented, we gain insight about the style that may feel most comfortable to us. I have met parents who feel they had wonderful parents and who plan to parent the same way. Others tell me they want to parent completely differently from the way they were parented, and some parents just want to change a few of the parenting methods they were raised with.

Before having children, it is beneficial for partners to discuss their families of origin and their respective parenting styles. When they do become new parents, the knowledge will help them to form a plan of how they want to parent their children. Two parents planning to raise children together may discover they have opposing ideas about values or methods of discipline. They will need to resolve their differences.

To parent well together, both parents will need to support one another and maintain consistency. Awareness, acceptance, and discussion about each other's parenting style will result in cohesive parenting. Solid teamwork will help to eliminate some of the manipulation techniques that children use when there is a lack of unity. Most parents have experienced a child asking, "Dad, can I have some ice cream?" Then the child adds, "Mom says it's okay with her." Later on, it may turn out that Mom said no such thing. Those parents who have taken the time to explore and share how they were parented will find it easier to form a strong and consistent team.

9

Styles of Parenting

When working with a group of parents, I usually start by identifying typical styles of parenting. The three most common parenting styles are autocratic, permissive, and democratic. Most parents recognize the style that feels most familiar to them.

The autocratic parent tends to give orders, likes rules and control, and uses rewards and punishments to motivate the child. "Brush your teeth now." "Get your backpack for school and put it in the car." What is this approach like for a child? Well, it does have structure, but the child doesn't learn how to take responsibility or to make decisions, because the parent does it all for them. Children with this type of parent seldom have to think for themselves.

The permissive parent is quite the opposite of the autocratic parent. With few rules and very little structure, this parent gives in to a child's demands easily. "Did you hear me? I said that it's bedtime." If the child starts to fuss or whine, the permissive parent gives in easily. "Well, all right, you can stay up for just one more TV show before bed." It may seem rather nice for children to get what they want without too much of a struggle, but in reality, it isn't. Children need some sense of order and routine in their lives to prepare them for the outside world.

The democratic parent is, of course, the perfect parent we all aspire to be. This parent sets limits, but also allows choices within the limits. "We're leaving for a walk in a little while. You can decide whether you want to wear your runners or your boots." This style of parenting fosters the child's developing independence by teaching responsibility.

Usually we can identify our own parenting style. I have found parents to be surprisingly honest in admitting that they know they are too bossy or too wishy-washy with their children. Being a perfect, democratic parent is not always easy, but we all have moments in our day when we do parent well.

What happens if our partner has an opposing parenting style from ours? Whose style should prevail? If both parents feel their way is the right way, their children will not know who to listen to. If Mom says, "Time for bed," and Dad says, "Oh, let them stay up a little longer" because he'd like to spend a bit more time with them, confusion will reign. Children will quickly learn to pit one parent against the other in order to get what they want. The world is made up of all sorts of different types of people. So it doesn't harm children when their parents have different styles, as long as the parents discuss their differences and stand together as a team on key issues of discipline and values.

However, one thing you don't want to do is to correct your partner's parenting in front of the children. Discuss those tricky issues in private.

10 Flip-Flop Parenting

Toolbox Skill

Be aware of your parenting style. Take note of what triggers you to flip-flop so you can be prepared for it next time.

Through my own parenting experience, I discovered a fourth style of parenting. While raising my three children, I studied parenting styles and took a look at my own approach. Rather smugly, I decided I was not too autocratic and not too permissive. Patting myself on the back, I deduced that through the process of elimination, I must be a perfect, democratic parent. It's amazing how the mind can override reality.

The next day I decided to observe myself in action with my three children. The first thing I noticed was that at the start of the day I was very autocratic, or what my children would call "bossy," issuing orders to all. "Everyone up. Time for breakfast. Cereal is on the menu today. Shoes on now! Let's go! Come on, everyone in the car." A string of commands spewed out of my mouth, and there was no room for argument or discussion from the children. I had an agenda, and everyone was going to meet it!

Interestingly, around 4 to 6 pm, during what are often called the "arsenic hours," a very different parent emerged. The children claimed they were hungry and wanted cookies. Maintaining some of my former strictness, I began with, "No, we're not having cookies now. It's almost supper time." This elicited a string of grumbles and whines from the children, and my firm resolve disappeared as I gave up the battle. "Fine, then, have cookies. Just stop your whining and, if you like, eat the whole box because I just don't care anymore." How mature was that?

When we're tired or frustrated, we may lack the energy to follow through with our usual parenting style. This is when we may exhibit a fourth style of parenting that I label "flip-flop" parenting. I was tired, frustrated, lacked energy, and consequently became very permissive. Most of us flip-flop somewhere between strict and lenient throughout the day. Oh, I should note that I did find a time when I really was able to be the perfect, democratic parent. It was when they were all asleep!

Flip-flop parenting is reassuringly human and normal, but we can still strive for improvement by being aware of how our behaviour impacts the children's behaviour. Children react to whatever style we present, and democratic parenting provides more stability for them.

11 Noticing Good Behaviour

There is another interesting behaviour that parents sometimes display. We pay absolutely no attention to our children when they are playing quietly by themselves, or interacting well with a sibling or friend. Of course, we all know why! It allows us time to catch up with the many chores, phone calls, and cooking that constantly await our attention. However, let's look at the flip side of that.

Toolbox Skill

Notice good behaviour and you'll get more.

When our children are bugging us or squabbling with each other, we dish out lots of attention to them by trying to change their unruly behaviour. It took me a while to figure out what was going wrong, but eventually I realized that when I noticed and paid attention to the good behaviour, I got more of it. Likewise, when I paid attention to unpleasant behaviour, I got more of that. The problem is that we tend to notice disruption more than peace.

Now, you are probably thinking to yourself, "But who would interrupt a child playing quietly in order to give them positive attention?" I absolutely agree. It would be foolish to ruin such a golden opportunity. However, when the peaceful moments are over, be sure to acknowledge them with an encouraging comment to show that you noticed, and appreciated, the behaviour. "Thanks for playing so nicely with your sister. That was a big help, and I've managed to get my chores done, so now let's go and have fun at the park."

Noticing the positive can also help to change a child's attitude. Our children used to take turns setting the table for dinner. The two older children set the table without complaint. When the youngest had his turn, he would moan and groan about how unfair it was that he should have to do such hard work. His whining nearly drove me to the point of saying that I would set the table for him. But I realized that was what he wanted and, that if I did, it wasn't fair to the other two children. I decided to try to give him some positive attention. It was not easy to find anything about table setting that he was doing well. In desperation, I said, "Wow! No one can put the cutlery down as quietly as you can. I can hardly hear a sound." The result was just like magic. Every time he put down a knife, fork, or spoon, he would ask, "Did you hear anything, Mom?" From then on, setting the table became something he liked to do, and we never had complaining again. I tucked that skill firmly in the front of my parenting toolbox.

12 Changing the Pattern

Each one of us has our own way of doing things, and we often fall into routines that work for us. As parents, we anticipate that our children will follow our routines. Sometimes, though, our routines don't work for our children. We lose sight of the fact that they are individuals wanting to find their own way of doing things. Imagine what it must be like to have someone always telling you what to do and when to do it.

A father in one of my parenting groups wanted to know what he could do to prevent the daily battle of getting his little girl's shoes on before leaving for afternoon preschool. I asked him to describe the routine he was using. He told me they had lunch together at noon, which they both enjoyed, and then it was time for a visit to the bathroom and putting shoes on for school. His daughter was four years old, and quite capable of getting her own shoes on. According to Dad, she would do anything rather than put her shoes on. She played with the straps, fiddled with other toys, sang little songs, and just would not hurry up and get her shoes on. Time would be slipping by and Dad, who was busy cleaning up the lunch things, would begin to urge her to hurry up so they wouldn't be late. Dad's growing frustration didn't inspire the little girl to hurry, and eventually he would put the shoes on for her. She didn't like that and would start to cry, resulting in both of them arriving for school upset.

I suggested changing the pattern by putting on the shoes before the enjoyable lunchtime. Dad looked at me in astonishment, said he hadn't thought of that, and that he'd give it a try. A week later, he arrived at the class with a huge grin on his face. Since he'd changed the routine around, things had improved. His daughter seemed quite happy to put her shoes on before lunch. There was no more unhappiness before they left for school, and he jokingly said that putting on shoes before lunch had changed his life.

Changing the pattern can be useful when daily routines are not working. It can solve some of the homework issues with school-age children. Parents often impose a homework time that just doesn't work well for the child. If the child is fidgety and unable to concentrate on homework after supper, try setting aside some time for homework before supper once the child has had a snack and some time to play or relax. Teenagers, too, may want to do more things their way as they mature. As long as their ideas don't affect the rest of the family or the family values, it's a good opportunity for them to learn that routines are important but not set in stone.

13 Being Flexible

For most situations with children, consistency is an important skill recommended by many parenting experts. But we also need to recognize that the world could not function if we were black and white with all our decisions. Children will need to learn that life does have gray areas. There are times when opportunities arise for us to show our children that being flexible can be acceptable at times.

Suppose your child is usually responsible about getting his school projects in on time. One day you receive a phone call from your tearful son, who has left his project at home and is begging you to bring it to school. Provided you are able to deliver the project, this situation presents an excellent opportunity to teach flexibility. You could tell your child, "You know, we all slip up sometimes, and since you are normally very responsible about your projects, I am glad to be able to help you out this time." Think how you would feel if you phoned home to ask your loved one to bring in an important work presentation you had left behind by mistake, and he refused, saying, "Well, that will teach you! You'll never make that mistake again." We've all had times when we needed rescuing, and our children are no exception.

Another situation warranting flexibility might be if out-of-town grandparents were visiting, and a child was allowed to reschedule a weekly piano lesson in order to have extra time with them. The parents would need to make sure the child knew that this was only possible because the visit was such a special occasion. Being flexible does not mean commitments are not honoured. However, they can sometimes be changed to suit the occasion.

It's Not A Plot To Drive You Crazy

14 Keeping Your Sense of Humour

Toolbox Skill

Use humour to keep your perspective. Have fun and laugh with your children.

Keep your sense of humour – parenting can be fun! We often take our job as parents very seriously and we forget to enjoy the journey. It is the humorous moments that lighten the load for parents. Laughter is a wonderful tonic for weary parents. Sometimes, it can be the silliest things that cause mirth.

The children and I were in the car one day, on the way to visit friends who lived across town. All three children were in the back seat and, after a while, there seemed to be a lot of giggling going on. Glancing in my rear view mirror, I noticed they were sticking their tongues out at passing motorists and thoroughly enjoying the reactions. Staring at the road ahead of me, I said firmly, "It is extremely rude to stick your tongues out at people, so please stop." There was absolute silence for a few seconds, and then one of the children whispered to the others, "How did she know what we were doing?" They couldn't understand how I knew what they were up to. I said, "Moms and Dads have eyes in the backs of their heads, as well as in the front." They hadn't realized that the rear view mirror allowed me to watch them, and their behaviour was greatly improved as we continued on our way. I found it hard to keep the grin off my face. Of course, the children soon figured out how I knew, but it was a wonderfully, funny moment, and I still chuckle when I remember it.

Humour can often help to diffuse a difficult situation. A child who is becoming frustrated with the struggle to put on a sock might respond to a parent who makes dressing fun. "Hmm. It looks as if Mr. Sock is in a bad mood today. Let's give him a little shake, and then he may feel better about going over your toes." Children love it when we make life fun, and are more likely to cooperate when some humour is added to a situation.

Older children, too, will often respond better to humour than to an angry parent. One parent told me about a furious argument she was having with her teenage daughter over the appropriate attire for going for dinner with her grandparents. Furiously, the teen said, "Well, if you won't let me wear that skirt, I won't wear anything." Mom, trying to use a bit of humour to avoid more conflict, laughingly said, "You know, I think that might give Grandma and Grandpa a bit of a shock, don't you?" After saying, "Oh gross, Mom!" her daughter couldn't help laughing at the thought of going to dinner without her clothes on. Some of the anger dissipated, and they managed to reach an amicable agreement. It is hard to continue to be angry when someone else is seeing the funny side of the situation.

Although humour can often diffuse a difficult situation, it works best when we use humour to laugh at ourselves rather than at the child. Children do tell us some very funny things and sometimes it is hard not to laugh, but it is also important not to demean their point of view.

15

Expectations

During one session of a parenting group, a mother of a two-year-old girl shared her experience. She had completed her homework assignment – to record the number of times she used the words "no" and "don't" during a normal day. She reported that, because of the assignment, she had paid more attention to what she said. She was quite taken aback when she had heard herself say in exasperation to her little girl, "Would you just quit acting like a child?" She then told us, "I couldn't believe I said that. How ridiculous! Of course she acts like a child – she is one."

As parents, we often have unrealistic expectations of our children. In fact, we often expect more from our own children than we would from other people's children, or even from other adults. Those of us with more than one child may find we place unreasonable demands on our eldest child, and that the youngest one gets away with too much, which can create sibling rivalry.

Parents make many assumptions about how much their children know. A young child uses a crayon to colour on the wall and the parent reacts with horror. But, perhaps the parent has omitted to explain to the child that crayons are only to be used on paper. Before reacting with annoyance, it is helpful to examine whether your expectations are realistic. Of course, if the child does know crayons don't go on walls, then the logical consequence is to take away the crayons for a while, or to allow them only to be used with adult supervision.

Our expectations of older children can also be unrealistic. I once overheard my nine-year-old son giving out some very personal family information to a telemarketer who was on the phone. At first I was annoyed with him, but then I realized he had been taught to be respectful to adults, and that he was doing just that. We had never explained that there were some exceptions to that rule.

It's Not A Plot To Drive You Crazy

As an analogy of how children view their world according to their age, imagine a window with many panes of glass in it. Adults are able to look through all the panes and have a clear view of what lies on the other side. At first, small children can only look through the very lowest panes, and then as they grow older, they are able to see through more and more of the panes. They can't see the whole picture, so they must rely on adults for that. Sometimes, parents forget children have limited visibility, and their expectations of children's abilities become too high.

It's important to stay abreast of developmental ages and stages when you are parenting. If we keep in mind the limited height of panes that a two year old, a nine year old, and a fifteen year old can look through, we may have more patience and understanding of realistic expectations.

16 Size Doesn't Equal Maturity

Toolbox Skill

Gauge expectations by maturity, not size.

We often base our expectations on the size of the child. We expect more from a tall three year old than from a short three year old, because we equate size with maturity. That equation does not apply fairly to children or to adults. I once worked for a very petite woman, whom I admired because of her progressive and dynamic approach to her job. It never occurred to me to wonder if her small stature might diminish her capabilities.

We often expect teens to think and reason like adults once they are adult-sized. Despite their grown-up appearance, we need to remember that their reasoning and logic are still underdeveloped. Teens are still figuring out and exploring the angles in life. They will experiment and test many limits during their adolescence. Despite the fact that many of them are taller than their parents, they still need parental wisdom, maturity, and guidance.

17

Try, Try Again!

My work at a Family Resource Centre includes teaching parenting skills to parents from many different cultures. One young mother, originally from Iran, attended almost every one of my different parenting sessions. She had a five-year-old son and a two-year-old daughter and, when we first met, she told me they were driving her crazy, and that she felt she was a terrible mother. Her son would not listen to her, and when she shouted at him to make him listen, it frightened her little daughter and then she would scream, too. Every day followed the same pattern, she told me, and they were all unhappy.

A few months later, I asked her if she was finding the parent education useful. She replied that she was learning a great deal about her parenting that had not made sense before. She was now trying to notice her children's positive behaviours and being more consistent in her reactions to them. She told me that when she tried the new skills initially, she became very frustrated and angry because her son's behaviour did not alter immediately. However, she persisted with the new skills, and gradually she began to notice some small changes. The most noticeable change was that her son began to listen and to respond to her calm voice, so she didn't need to shout at him so much. His reaction to her new approach encouraged her to keep trying. Now, she had a new set of skills that helped her to feel more confident about her parenting, her children were more cooperative, and there was more harmony in their relationship. When I commended her on her persistence, she simply replied, "It was worth it, because now we are all so much happier."

As my own mother used to say, "If at first you don't succeed, try, try again." That adage is most apt with parenting. We all like to find a quick fix or an instant solution for most issues. When we try a new parenting approach, we often expect an instant change in the child. Yet children have learned their responses over time, so it is to be expected that any change will take time to work. Children are very fixed in their routines, so even when a change is for the better, they may feel some confusion and uncertainty, wanting us to revert back to the old ways. They may even behave worse than usual, just to see if they can shift us off the new track. If only we could all have the same determination that the young Iranian mother showed – to keep trying, with the conviction that it will be worth it in the end.

We will spend many hours perfecting a golf swing, trying out recipes, or taking courses to improve our knowledge. Parenting takes time and effort, too. The attempts to change become worthwhile, because our efforts are usually rewarded with good results.

18

Mom! Mom!

Toolbox Skill

Keep a log of funny events that happen when parenting. It's so easy to forget, and later on, children enjoy hearing stories about themselves.

This little story is for all the mothers who get so tired of hearing the word Mom, over and over again. We all get worn down by the incessant calling for us. Sometimes when our children yell for their Mom, they can't even remember what they wanted. They just want to connect with us, but it's enough to drive even the most patient parents insane.

One day, when our children were all under the age of seven, I recall listening to what seemed like a constant barrage of "Mom!" Towards late afternoon, as we entered the arsenic hours, my frustration got the better of me. I said firmly to my little ones, "That's enough. I don't want to hear the word 'Mom' from any of you for the rest of the day." There was total silence, as they contemplated this difficult task. Then a little voice said with complete sincerity, "Shall we call you Fran, instead?"

19

Grandparents

Toolbox Skill

Value grandparents and the important role they play in our children's lives. Grandparents can help parents by giving them encouragement and support.

For those families lucky enough to have them around, grandparents play a vital role in children's lives. Grandparents are not as busy as parents. They no longer have both career and family to balance, so they often have more time and patience to listen to children and play with them. On the whole, the importance of grandparents seems undervalued by our society. Grandparents often provide support for the whole family, who benefit from their wisdom and deep understanding of life. They have many important roles, including those of historians and guides. Most families these days need both parents out in the workforce to make ends meet, and many grandparents are playing an active role in helping out with child care. This can be a bonus for all concerned, as long as no one feels taken for granted.

How to handle difficulties with grandparents is a question that is often raised in my parenting groups. Interference, unwanted advice, and criticism of parenting by grandparents are the most common causes for complaint. Examining differences in parenting styles and family values can be a useful exercise for parents, to provide a better understanding of why grandparents act the way they do. There are ways that compromise can be reached, so that parents, grandparents, and the grandchildren can all enjoy their times together.

Parents should be prepared for grandparents to be more lenient with their children than they themselves are. Most grandparents firmly believe they have earned the right to spoil their grandchildren, and will do so, even if the parents object. Some grandparents have learned from experience which battles to fight with children, while others are a bit out of practice and may have forgotten the basic rules of setting limits. If parents are prepared to leave their children with grandparents, they should also accept that once they leave, the grandparents' rules are what the children will follow. If those rules are unacceptable to the parents, perhaps they need to consider alternative child care. It is the unconditional love that grandparents provide for their grandchildren that is so nurturing. Grandparents provide a solid foundation of love on which children can build confidence and the courage to try new things.

If you're a grandparent you will promote good relations with your children, and your grandchildren, by encouraging and supporting your adult children as they parent. They are doing the best parenting job they can. Use behaviour, not words, to model your ways of doing things that work with the children, and your adult children may adopt those methods when they see the benefits. It is the rare occasion when unsolicited advice is welcome. Parents are far more likely to accept your advice when they request it than when you offer it. Most importantly, when your grandchildren's parents are present, it should be their rules that take precedence, since they are the primary caregivers.

Children catch on very fast as to what is allowed and with whom. They can adapt to differences in rules from household to household more easily than we anticipate. Confusion for children only occurs when parents and grandparents are competing with one another. My parents always used to tell me our children behaved best once we were out of the way, probably because the children then knew exactly whose rules took precedence.

PART 2

Tools For The Trying Times

20 Out in Public

Parents who are doing a fine job of parenting at home may find their skills fall apart when out in public or visiting family. It is so much easier to deal with tantrums or misbehaviour within the confines of home than in a public place with lots of people watching. A child experiencing a tantrum is rather like a car alarm. A lot of noise turns heads and attracts attention. Unfortunately, the public is often more critical of parents than they are supportive. As a parent struggling with a difficult child, you'd appreciate a sympathetic smile, a word of support, or an offer to push the grocery cart much more than comments about how you ought to be dealing with your child. Since most parents are trying to do their best, support from other adults in public will help to create more of a community approach to raising the next generation.

Here are some tips that other parents have found useful when they are out in public:

- Be sure your expectations of behaviour have been clearly communicated to the child, and give some idea of how long the errand will take. "We're going to the bank because I need some money. I'd like you to help me by staying close to me so that we can be as quick as possible, and then we can go to Grandma's for supper."

- Choose a time for excursions when energy levels are high. Avoid these trips when your child is tired or hungry. It's so much easier to get things done when everyone is in a good mood.

Toolbox Skill

Take your parenting toolbox with you wherever you go, to help you maintain consistency.

- Be consistent with your parenting skills. Try to respond to your child as you would at home. Children know when you are behaving differently, and will test the limits because they don't understand why.

- Take a snack or a special toy for those inevitable delays or lineups.

- Involve your child whenever possible. My children used to enjoy filling in bank slips and handing them to the teller. The teller usually found it amusing, thanking them profusely. Many parents will take the time to let their little ones push the buttons on elevators, or to help pick out fruit and vegetables when shopping for produce. Yes, it takes more time, but not as much as you'll need if the child falls apart.

- Going to a restaurant with very small children can be a frustrating exercise. Sometimes it is worth waiting until they are older and can sit for longer periods of time. If you do go, choose child-friendly restaurants and take a good supply of crayons and paper.

- Follow through with promised consequences. If you are in a restaurant, and have warned the child that if his behaviour doesn't improve you will have to leave, then you must leave if the behaviour doesn't change. It is important to show children that we mean what we say, and follow through. Eventually the child won't need to test the limits to know that you mean what you say.

- Remind any criticizing family members that you are doing your best with your parenting, and that you need their support more than their advice. Using clear "I" statements can help with this tricky message. "*I* realize that you don't always agree with some of my child-raising methods. *I* am parenting in the way that works best for my family, and *I'd* very much appreciate your support."

21 Pick-Up Problems

Toolbox Skill

Before picking up children, give them some advance warning so they can be prepared both emotionally and physically for your arrival.

Many working parents have told me that picking up little ones from their child care location at the end of the day can be a particularly trying experience. After being away from our children all day, we look forward to seeing them and to getting home. We anticipate that the children, too, will be delighted to see us, and that they'll give us a big welcome hug and cooperate fully in getting ready to come home. Often, the opposite happens. The child kicks up a huge fuss about having to leave, and is carried out to the car kicking and screaming, with the caregiver muttering, "I don't understand it. She's been an angel all day." Not exactly what the poor parent needs to hear at that moment.

It helps to look at this from a different angle, so that we can understand what this is like for the child. If she had no idea when her parent was going to show up, she may be unhappy about having to leave. Perhaps she was in the middle of a fun activity. Let's imagine what this might be like if it happened to an adult. Picture yourself watching a good movie on TV, when suddenly your beloved appears and says, "Come on. We've got to leave right now. Hurry up, let's get going." I suspect our reaction to these sudden commands would be anger and resentment. Some prior warning would have been appreciated. We would feel rushed and disrespected, as well as disappointed that we could not finish watching the movie.

Children are constantly subjected to the invisible timing and scheduling imposed by their parents. They, like us, are more willing to cooperate with the leaving process if they are given some advance warning. If the parent always arrives to pick the child up at a set time, perhaps the caregiver could inform the child as the time draws near, even putting on her coat and shoes to prepare her for leaving. If the time of arrival varies from day to day, the parent could call the caregiver before leaving work, or could use a cell phone to give an estimated time of arrival.

22 Sharing

Sharing does not come naturally to children. The concept of sharing needs to be taught, and there are several different levels of sharing. The beginning stage for toddlers is to learn to take turns with other children. This can involve taking turns with toys at home, at daycare, and at the playground. At the same time, the child is also learning that we don't share the food on our plate. Yet, sometimes they see a plate of sandwiches being handed around. Isn't that sharing food on a plate? Imagine how confused a little child can become, with so many conflicting messages about how to share.

Developmentally, toddlers are busy mastering the concept of *me* and *mine*, having just made the discovery that they are individuals and not extensions of their parents. These little ones want to own almost everything they see and touch, so teaching them how to take turns is not an easy task. The concept of ownership needs to be experienced before a toddler is ready to take turns. Parents can help by modelling ownership and sharing. "These glasses belong to Daddy. Thank you for giving them to me." After doing a puzzle together, "You shared your puzzle with me, and I had fun doing it with you."

The next stage is to help children learn that sharing sometimes involves relinquishing their toys to a visiting friend. I recommend encouraging visiting friends to bring some of their own toys along, so that both children are involved in the sharing process. Before another child comes over to play, invite your child to put away anything he doesn't feel like sharing that day. Often, small children have a new or favourite toy that is just too special to share. By giving the child permission to put away the most favourite toys, we encourage the sharing of all the other toys, and sometimes the child will even bring back into play the removed possessions. Some parents have expressed the fear that their child would put everything away, and that there would be nothing to play with. I think this possibility is highly unlikely, but if it did happen, I'm sure the children would be innovative enough to find something to have fun with, or else they would learn – no toys means no fun!

Children learn how to share by observing what adults do. Let them see you sharing your possessions and being kind to others. It's important for our children to be a part of helping others in need. Being involved in community efforts that help others can show children of all ages that giving is often as rewarding as receiving.

It's Not A Plot To Drive You Crazy

Children in elementary school are busy discovering what is fair and not fair in life. Within the family, teach the older children the part of sharing that involves borrowing. It is most unfair when someone takes your things without asking. Older children need to learn that when you borrow, you ask first, and it is your responsibility to return what you borrowed.

Teens are also able to embrace the more abstract ideas of sharing, like understanding the gift of time when a parent helps with driving practice or assists with a school project. The teen can learn to give back, perhaps by helping with extra chores.

Even adults still retain a bit of the *me* and *mine* stage. I must confess that I have a special coffee mug that I use every day. It is exclusively mine. No one in my family is allowed to use it, and it is never offered to guests. A quirk of mine, perhaps, or maybe a throwback to my own childhood.

23 Mealtime

Mealtime is another topic that invariably comes up in the question periods in my classes. I hear comments and questions like:

"Last week my child loved broccoli, this week she won't touch it."

"Our evening meal has become a nightmare."

"How long should our child be sitting at the table?"

"I ask my son what he would like to eat, but when I make what he wants for supper he still won't eat it."

Parents worry constantly about mealtime. I am not a nutritionist, so this parenting tool is not about what children eat, but about setting limits for mealtime behaviour.

Parents of younger children seem to have the most concerns about eating habits. Unless they have an eating disorder, most school-age children and teens eat well, guided by their feelings of hunger. Small children's appetites, however, seem to fluctuate dramatically. Sometimes they eat lots and at other times, they suddenly become very picky. A child's eating schedule often differs from that of an adult. Parents have told me they find that small children eat better and seem more hungry at breakfast and lunch than at the evening meal. Many families plan a healthy evening meal and expect that everyone will sit together, behave well, and enjoy some pleasant family time together. Typically this does not work with very young children, because it is not a prime eating time for them and it is often too late in the day. Evening meals can become a testing time, with children reacting to parental expectations that they behave well and eat nicely.

Mealtime and the whole issue of food can become difficult because children are in control of their own eating. Children easily pick up on our anxiety about the quantity and quality of food they eat, and then the battles begin. Even if we are frustrated and angry, we cannot make them eat. It may help to remember that the parent's responsibility is to supply nutritious food; the child's responsibility is to eat.

Not all families can manage the "let's all eat together at suppertime" routine. My family gave it up while we had three children under five years of age. The children had a good breakfast and their main meal was at lunchtime, followed by an early, light supper. We adults sat down together, either after the children were in bed or after they had eaten their own supper. The children could listen to stories on tape, watch a video, or play together, while we enjoyed a short but civilized meal, catching up on our respective days. By the time they went to elementary school, they wanted to eat with us in the evenings, and could manage to sit through a later suppertime.

It's Not A Plot To Drive You Crazy

Of course, this may be difficult for working parents who only have the evening with their children and may not be able to feed the little ones early. Taking turns may work best for these parents. One can play with the children while the other makes dinner, then they can switch the next day. It also helps if you can be prepared by having a couple of meals in the freezer, ready for re-heating on those days when you are running late and everyone is starving. I found a Crock-Pot useful, but it means an earlier start to the day for chopping and preparing the ingredients.

Some ideas and successful tips for pleasant mealtimes include:

- Give children small amounts of food. They can always have more, and large amounts can be overwhelming.

- Serve food smorgasbord-style whenever possible and let them help themselves. Parents are responsible for making sure the selection provides a nutritious and balanced diet. "You can choose two things you like and I will put one spoonful of each on your plate, and then I get to choose one more for you." Children will be more likely to eat food they have helped to choose.

- Encourage children to sample new foods and have faith that as they grow older, they will become more adventurous in their eating.

- Most two to five year olds can only sit at the table for 10 to 15 minutes at a time.

- If children play with their food, the meal is over! Remove the food calmly, saying, "I see you are finished." If the child protests, allow one, but only one, more chance.

- If children are hungry between meals, a plate of raw vegetables for snacking may fill the void and won't spoil their appetites.

- Try not to become a short-order cook, preparing different meals for each child. Most of us do not have time to cater to individual tastes. Encourage your children to try different foods. Don't worry if they won't eat. Offer the raw vegetables and they will probably be hungry for the next meal.

- Beware of the "I'm hungry" message. Small children discover that when they say, "I'm hungry," their parents leap into action to solve the problem. Sometimes a child is not hungry, but bored or wanting attention.

- When they really were hungry and they have eaten well, give them the correct vocabulary. "My goodness, you were very hungry, but now I think you're feeling full." Children need to connect the feelings of being hungry and being full with the corresponding words.

- A little food at a time, spread out regularly through the day, seems to work best for small children.

- Encourage healthy attitudes about food, and eating.

Too much attention paid to eating can cause a problem. An anxious mother complained to me that her child ate virtually nothing, and she was desperately worried about her. This mother admitted she cajoled, changed the menu, and tried everything to persuade the child to eat. At the time, she and I were chatting in a Family Resource Centre, and snack was about to be served to the children. Mom assured me that her little girl would eat nothing. The little girl did not look undernourished, so I wondered if perhaps Mom was overly concerned about her child's eating habits. I asked Mom to engage in conversation with me, and to sit with her back to her child while snack was served. I watched the child. As soon as the bowls of snack appeared, the little girl looked for Mom, and noticed that she was close by but that her attention was elsewhere. The child watched the other children eating busily and, after a few seconds, started to eat her own snack. Not only did she finish it, but she asked the staff for more. Mom learned a lot from this experience and, a week later, after paying a lot less attention and being more relaxed at mealtime, reported back that her little one seemed to have developed a much better appetite.

24 Bedtime

Parents of young children often find themselves longing for that magic moment when the children are tucked into bed. At last, the adults can have some time to themselves, to relax, or catch up with all the things that can't be done while children are around. Parents want bedtime to be pleasant for all, but if they are too eager to get the children into bed, they may convey a sense of urgency to their children. Children notice the parents' urgency and become unsettled, turning peaceful bedtime routines into a battlefield. Sometimes they go to bed, only to appear every few minutes needing this or that, which can drive parents almost to insanity. When the bedtime routine goes smoothly, children settle happily and their parents can enjoy a few hours to themselves without the guilt and exhaustion that follows a bedtime battle.

The following suggestions may help to make bedtimes more pleasant and peaceful for children and their tired parents:

- Respect your own needs by taking care of yourself during the day so that you are not feeling too frazzled by bedtime.

- Decide on a bedtime ritual or routine that you can follow every night. Children like order in their lives, and are more likely to oblige when they know what happens next. Explain the bedtime routine to anyone putting your children to bed. Consistency is crucial. The wonderful part is that the routine is portable and can be used when on vacation or staying with relatives. Take it with you in your toolbox.

- Start the bedtime routine at least half an hour before the actual time you want the child to be in bed. This should be a winding down time, so avoid all rowdy activities. Many parents find dimming the lights and putting on some soft music helps to set the mood. You may find yourself yawning, too!

- Respect the child's sense of timing by letting him know bedtime is getting closer. Allow time for an activity to be completed, or help the child to put what he is doing in a safe place until the next morning.

- Whenever possible, involve both parents in the bedtime routine. It can be an enjoyable family activity. For those times when only one parent is taking care of bedtime, it is important for the other to stay away and not be manipulated by the child saying. "I want Daddy/Mommy to put me to bed, not you."

- Create an ending to bedtime. Read a story, have a kiss and hug, then leave the room, singing a goodnight song or a little rhyme. Be clear that this is the end, and do the same thing every night to provide a sense of closure and security.

- Children who stay up too late because they are not tired may need their afternoon nap eliminated or shortened. It is hard to wake them from a deep sleep in the afternoon, and you need to decide if you prefer to deal with a grouchy child who needs an earlier bedtime, or a child who has had a good nap and wants to be up late. You may also want to discuss shortening or removing naps with your child's caregiver.

- Sometimes children wonder if they are missing out on a big party after they have been put to bed. If a child gets up, let him see that most nights you are having quiet, peaceful times, and that might help to make his bed seem a little more attractive.

- On the nights that you do have company, expect your children to be curious and allow a little flexibility about bedtime.

- For children who constantly get up to find the parents and just can't seem to settle, try putting a chair outside the child's bedroom and sitting there with a good book or some paper work. Children sometimes feel nervous when they are left alone, and are reassured by a parent being close at hand. Let the child know that you are there but not for chatting, and that it is time to be quiet. Each night, move a little farther away as the child feels more secure. It usually takes about a week, and then you can let them know you will check on them every 15 minutes. Be sure to do so. Once they know you will do as you say, they will relax and fall asleep.

- Some children don't like the dark, so a dimmer switch or nightlight in the hallway can be comforting.

- Many parents complain about a child coming to their bed in the wee hours and disturbing their sleep. If this is not something you want to happen, make up a little bed on the floor by your bed. Show the child what you have done and tell him, if he needs you in the night, that the bed is there for him so he will be close to you. The first night, this may take some persuasion. Be firm, and tell the child he can sleep there beside you, or go back to his own bed. After a while, most children don't bother to get up, as their own bed is more comfortable.

It's Not A Plot To Drive You Crazy

25 Screen Time

I am frequently asked questions about TV and computer time. How much screen time should children have? Which shows should be avoided? Is violence in cartoons as harmful as real life shows with violence?

Here are some tips gathered from the experiences of other parents and teachers that may help with screen time issues:

• Insist your children take frequent breaks from watching TV. Because TV watching is a passive activity, it stifles natural movement and creativity, and children, especially young ones, need to be on the move. I noticed that my two young sons became very aggressive towards each other after a long spell of TV watching. When the TV was turned off, their imaginations about how to amuse themselves seemed also to be switched off. Annoying each other became the sport of the moment. I limited screen time to an hour a day when they were under seven and insisted on physical activity afterwards. Rain or shine, a good run outside always seemed to help diminish any aggression.

• Avoid early morning screen time. Many preschool teachers have told me they notice that children who come into the classroom after watching early morning TV have a harder time settling down than the children who don't. Encourage your children to play on their own before school rather than watching TV or sitting in front of the computer. Most children are happy to have play time first thing in the morning, when they are well rested and full of creative juices. If screen time is not an option, they will find other things to do.

• Try not to use TV as a babysitter while you get dressed and ready for your own day. Many parents fall into this habit, then avoid a fuss by letting their children eat breakfast in front of the TV. Food seems to go down more easily with visual distraction. Unfortunately, these patterns are hard to break, and children may come to associate watching TV with food and snacks, which opens up a whole new set of problems!

• Get up earlier than your child. This is an unpopular suggestion with most parents, who value every minute of their sleep. But if parents are dressed and ready, they do have more patience, and don't need the TV to keep children out of the way. As your reward, you might want to enjoy the morning paper and a hot drink before the children get up.

• Watch what they watch. Whenever possible, be aware of the subject matter your children are watching. Some of the values shown on television may conflict with your values. Some of the content may need discussion.

• When in doubt about the content, turn the TV off. This is where our gut instinct can be a good indicator of what is inappropriate viewing material. Of course, your children will protest, especially school-age children and teens. They will tell you that they already know all about "that stuff." Use this as a teachable moment to explain that some programs go against your values. Not only does this give you a chance to reiterate your values, but it also gives you and your children the opportunity to send a message to the programmers. This approach seems to be more acceptable to children. The key is to know what they watch and be selective.

- Encourage good viewing There are some excellent family and educational programs, and when parents watch with their children, opportunities for learning and discussion often arise.

- Use caution with cartoons. Most young children seem to know the difference between animation and real life, but if you feel your child is unsure, it may be best to avoid cartoons until he is a little older.

26 Lying or "It Wasn't Me!"

"My child has started to lie to me. What can I do to stop the lies?" Parents are usually shocked by their child's first lies. Perhaps they fear that their child will become a serial liar. Lying seems to start around the age of four. Fortunately for parents, when small children lie, it is usually extremely obvious. However, sometimes our response to a child's misbehaviour creates a situation where the child feels the need to lie to stay out of trouble.

Toolbox Skill

Role model and encourage honesty. State the obvious, and help children to learn the importance of telling the truth.

Let's say, for example, the parent returns to the living room and finds a broken vase on the floor. The possible suspects? A baby and a four year old who've been left alone for a few seconds. The four year old says that the baby broke it. The parent knows perfectly well that the baby, who is not even crawling, couldn't have broken it, and responds: "Don't be silly. The baby couldn't reach that vase. You broke it, didn't you?" When parents overreact to a lie by accusing instead of stating the facts, this may set up the child to lie again.

Let's look at this from the child's point of view. By the age of four, most children have experienced a fairly noticeable reaction from parents when something is knocked over or broken. So, when the vase breaks, the child is shaken by the damage and fears the parent's reaction. It is understandable that when faced with an angry-looking parent, the child will feel scared and may try to divert the parent's wrath away from himself by not owning up to what he has done. This is not a deliberate or premeditated lie, but rather an attempt to avoid what might come next.

It's Not A Plot To Drive You Crazy

The parent already knows that the older child must be the culprit, so needs to deal with the facts rather than setting up the scene for another lie. A child, when accused, will feel cornered and will likely try to deny it. It is better if the parent, recognizing that an accident has happened, engages the child in making amends, rather than placing too much focus on the lie. Encourage the truth by saying, "I'm really disappointed my vase is broken, but I'm glad you and the baby are all right. It helps when I know what really happened." Calmly suggest that you clear up the broken vase together. Since the pieces are probably sharp, the child could hold the dustpan while you sweep up the pieces.

Parents' reactions can often increase the lie. Mom, on the phone to a friend, sees her six-year-old daughter wander into the room with scissors in her hand, missing chunks of her hair. Mom is horrified and, in a loud voice, exclaims to the person on the other end of the phone, "I've got to go. Susie has cut her hair!" Mom now turns to Susie and, using an angry, accusing tone, says, "You cut your hair, didn't you?" Mom already knows what Susie has done, but wants Susie to own up to her dastardly deed. Susie, now worried by Mom's reaction and feeling cornered, tries to avoid more trouble by saying, "No, I didn't do it. Jenny did it." Susie's friend Jenny, however, has not been over to visit that day. Now Mom becomes even angrier, because Susie is making the lie even worse.

When children lie, it is often to avoid being punished. They may be uncertain of what will happen if they tell the truth. By forcing a confession from our child, we back them into a corner. We open the door to a lie. As children get older, parents who have overreacted to earlier lies may be setting the stage for more creative lies. We need to state what we think has happened. There may still be anger and consequences, but children will not be as tempted to lie if they trust their parents to be fair when the truth is told.

Sometimes we ourselves don't always set a good example when it comes to lying. On occasion we may tell fibs, forgetting that our children overhear and absorb everything we do and say. For example, when we ask a family member to tell an unwanted caller on the phone that we are not home, the children are confused because they see that we are home. Distinguishing between different levels of lies is too difficult for children.

27 Tattling

Tattling is another behaviour that parents dislike. We don't like it when a child attempts to get a sibling or friend into trouble. Tattling is often used by school-age children who are in the developmental stage of figuring out what is fair or unfair. Our reaction may be dismissive of the tattler, shooing her and her story away. Another time we may listen to the story and then leap into the fray to sort things out. If a child is in danger of being hurt, we may be grateful to the tattler. With all these different parental reactions, it is difficult for children to know when to tell and when not to tell.

Because of the possibility that a child could be revealing something important, it is a good idea to listen to a tattler. If Mary's trying to get her brother into trouble, you could try listening to her story carefully. Then ask Mary what she feels she could do about it and encourage her to think of ways to sort it out herself. You may have to give her a couple of suggestions. Since she's not successful at getting her brother into trouble, she'll probably run off to play again.

This can be a lengthy process to begin with, but it ensures that the parent hears of possible safety issues and avoids hasty reactions to tattling, which can result in more tattling.

28 Rewards and Bribes

Toolbox Skill

Rewards after good behaviour work better than bribes to get good behaviour.

Rewards are wonderful when deserved. I must admit that I love them, too, and who doesn't enjoy a bonus or treat after a success? The key with children is to try to reward successes, rather than setting up expectations. We are sometimes tempted to bribe a child to behave well. "If you sit quietly while we get groceries, I'll buy you some candy when we're finished." The child will then expect candy every time you buy groceries. The reward has now become an expectation.

It makes more sense to reward good behaviour than to bribe children to behave. It is best not to give predictable rewards after a routine event like grocery shopping. It works better to make an announcement such as, "It's been such a good day. You've played so nicely, and all my work is done. I think we deserve to go out for ice cream."

I'm often asked about the concept of spoiling children, and my response is that we all need to be spoiled once in a while. The key is "once in a while." A spoiled child is one who always gets what he wants. Look at this through adult eyes. Do we enjoy being spoiled? Of course we do, and as long as it doesn't become an expectation or a demand, then being spoiled occasionally is fine. Parents often worry about grandparents allowing children treats and privileges that may not be permitted at home. Usually this is an unnecessary worry, because children learn very quickly that there are different rules in different places.

29 Chores

Toolbox Skill

Involve children in appropriate household chores. Shared family chores teach important teamwork skills.

"If chores aren't done, then should we give children allowances?" I am often asked this question by parents. I believe chores and allowances are two separate issues, which teach children different concepts. Allowances teach children the basics of fiscal responsibility. Chores teach children how to contribute to the family team, and help children develop a sense of belonging within their family.

Let's start with the issue of chores. Chores are a fact of life for every family and each member of the family can help, according to their age and ability. We wouldn't ask a two year old to wash the floor, but we might teach him to hold a dustpan while someone older sweeps dirt into it. A nine year old can generally manage to tidy her room, but a three year old would need the task broken down into smaller tasks. "You pick up your books, while I make the bed." Younger children may need to work alongside an adult or older sibling to get their chores done. This teaches them how cooperation works, and doesn't overwhelm them with a task that is too large.

Adults might think that chores are a bore, but small children love to help and imitate their parents, and are more interested in the process of doing the task than in the end result. I remember my sister-in-law being horrified that at mealtime we would ask our baby son, who had just started walking, to get his high chair. He was able to push it to the table, and he knew that this task meant food was coming. This was not a chore for him, but an exciting event! Let's help children to think of chores as exciting events for as long as we can. Our attitude and appreciation helps to get chores done. Chores can even be fun if you play music or sing while you work.

Some parents can't bear to see an imperfect job. If you must redo the task, try to make sure your young child doesn't notice. The "doing" is more important than the result. But if an older child has done a sloppy job and you know he could do better, then it is appropriate to ask him to redo it. State clearly what needs to be done to avoid being hooked into an argument, and then leave him to get on with it. If he refuses, then tell him he can't do anything else until the chore has been completed.

It's Not A Plot To Drive You Crazy

Here is a story about our son Nick at age fourteen, and his chore of cleaning the bathroom. He gave his permission for me to share this anecdote.

One Saturday morning, I suggested Nick and I would each clean one of our two bathrooms, and then go out for lunch once we were finished. Nick readily agreed to this plan (too readily, in hindsight), and I busied myself with toilet brush and sponge, happy in the knowledge we were working as a team. I could hear water running in the other bathroom, so assumed my son was getting on with his task. After about fifteen minutes, I noticed that I could still hear the sound of water from Nick's bathroom, and decided to investigate. The door to the bathroom was shut and he didn't hear me as I opened it. There, perched happily on the closed toilet seat, was Nick, engaged in an intense game on his Game Boy. Meanwhile, the bath water gushed out of the tap, fooling his unsuspecting mother into thinking he was hard at work. Of course I was absolutely dumbfounded, but luckily my sense of humour kicked in before anger did. The look of guilt on Nick's face when he suddenly looked up and saw me was so funny that I laughed and said, "Oops, I think you are found out. We'll have to have sandwiches at home for lunch, and I'll take your Game Boy for the rest of the weekend." I left the bathroom without asking for further explanation or comment. You can imagine the cleaning frenzy that ensued. I ended up with two things – a good laugh and a very clean bathroom!

Had I reacted with anger, I suspect my son would have become defensive and rude in order to save face. Here was a situation where I knew what had happened and didn't need to ask. I just stated what I saw, and imposed the consequences of cancelling our lunch plans and removing his Game Boy. Seeing the humour in the situation helped me to keep my anger at bay. Interestingly, Nick has since told me that my lack of anger and calm reaction actually made him feel worse for trying to dupe me.

As the children get older, they can begin to sort out schedules and chores for themselves. Our three children used to argue incessantly about whose turn it was to ride in the middle seat of the car. After a family meeting to discuss their constant bickering, they decided that whoever had the weekly chore of setting the table for dinner would also ride in the middle seat for that week. My daughter, the eldest child, soon had a schedule drawn up and posted on the fridge, and arguing about the middle seat was never an issue again.

30 Allowances

Toolbox Skill

Allowances help children to learn how to budget and save.

Many parents grapple with the question "Should my child earn her allowance, or be given it?" I believe allowances work better to teach the concept of fiscal responsibility than to pay for chores. Although many parents do find it very tempting to withhold allowance to ensure chores are done, this can become a controlling and punitive measure, which in time may cause resentment and frustration.

The amounts for allowances paid to children will be up to each individual family to determine. Allowances help children to learn the difference between spending and saving. Parents can help children to formulate a plan as to how much of their allowance they will spend and how much they will save.

Discuss with your children what their allowance should cover and what you will pay for. Try not to rescue them when they have used up all their allowance on candy and want to go to a movie but have no money. If teens with a clothing and entertainment allowance have spent it all on entertainment, it's important for them to realize that the pair of jeans they absolutely "must have" must wait. It's wise not to lecture them about financial responsibility. Some lessons are hard enough to learn.

31 Manners

Toolbox Skill

Teach and role model manners. Children like to know how to behave.

Many years ago, we were on a plane trip with our four-year-old daughter. She liked to visit the airplane bathroom often, and raced off for one last visit before we landed. Near the end of a pregnancy, I waddled rather more slowly down the aisle after her. Suddenly, a man also in the aisle stopped me and said, "Is that your child?" Slightly apprehensive, I admitted that she was. To my amazement, he commented on how impressed he was with her manners. Apparently, as she raced by him, she brushed his arm and said, "Excuse me." My initial reaction had been to think, "Oh, no! What has she done?" We had consistently expected and taught good manners at home and I shouldn't have been surprised.

Our children need to learn politeness and respect at home, so that they can function with confidence in the adult world. It is hard work to keep reminding young children to say "please", "thank you," and "excuse me" at the appropriate times, but consistently expecting good manners is worth the effort. We all love it when someone comments on how well mannered our child is.

Another question that arises about manners is what to do when children refuse to greet family members or friends. Some parents are very embarrassed by this behaviour. They feel it appears rude and reflects badly on their ability to parent. If the parent becomes annoyed with the child, that gives him lots of negative attention. The result is more of the same behaviour. When we notice negative attention, we often get more of it.

This kind of situation can leave parents feeling quite powerless. It is impossible to force words out of a child's mouth except by using threats, and those don't work in the long term. Try role-playing with the child before an anticipated visit. You could say, "Let's pretend you are Grandma and I'm you. I've come to visit you and this is what I say, 'Hi Grandma, we've brought you some cookies.'" Then let the child practise. It may not work the first few times, but you can say in front of Grandma, "We've been practising greeting you." If you can, try a visit again soon, encouraging the use of the greeting. Children do like to know how to behave properly, and low-key encouragement works best.

Older children also need to be taught appropriate manners. I have always tried to teach mine that when visiting at a friend's house, they should seek out the adult and acknowledge them with a greeting. I must have done a thorough job, because I've heard my children on occasion say to their visiting friends, "Oh, by the way, my Mom likes it if you say 'Hi' to her." I also feel it is important for the adults to help young visitors to feel more comfortable by letting them know the house rules.

Often we've had teenage visitors in the house who won't even make eye contact with me, let alone greet me. Much to my children's embarrassment, I always make a point of respectfully greeting them and asking their name and a few questions. I'm trying to model the behaviour I would like back. There have been many rewarding moments when a non-communicative teen acknowledges me for the first time, after all my attempts to make contact. Even our children have celebrated those breakthroughs. The fun part, now that my children's friends are young adults, is that they will sit and chat with me.

At each stage of development, it is important to teach children appropriate behaviour so that they feel confident facing new social situations. My sense is that some children and teens get into trouble socially not because they are "bad kids," but because they really don't know how to behave and are uncomfortable in certain situations and around adults. It does take time to teach manners and appropriate behaviours, but we all benefit if we make the time. Politeness and respect are important life skills that enhance the whole community.

32 Vacationing or "Are We There Yet?"

Occasionally I am asked for tips on holidaying with children. My first response with parents of children under two years of age is, "Don't. Stay home and wait until they are older." Not very helpful advice, but it is so hard travelling with little ones. Trying to hush a crying baby in a hotel room is a nightmare I'd rather avoid. Then there is all their gear, from diapers to favourite toys to special foods.

Toolbox Skill

Prepare well in advance for vacations. Then you can relax and have fun.

Realistically, though, we do need to get away or visit family sometimes, so here are some tips that may help:

- A month or so before your departure date, start collecting snack foods, audio tapes, books, and little inexpensive toys, to provide an endless supply of surprises.

- Make a large note so that you don't forget any favourite teddies or blankets. If possible, buy extras in case of loss.

- On car trips, try to stop often at a park or a place where little legs can be well exercised.

- If you have to stay overnight in a motel, do some research and find a child-friendly spot with a pool or a play area, so the children have a chance to exercise before bedtime. When children are happy, their parents will be happy, too.

It's Not A Plot To Drive You Crazy

- Leave early in the day, when the children are refreshed and temperatures are cooler. Stop early, so you can all get an early night.

- Pillows in the car help children fall asleep. If they do sleep, enjoy the peaceful moments, and keep driving!

- In planes, use the aisles for exercise whenever possible, and don't worry about the other passengers. Most of them enjoy seeing little ones around.

- Try to request a bulkhead seat where there is a little more floor space. It usually means you can't see the movie, but what were the chances that you'd see it anyway?

- Always take a complete change of clothes for the children, and, if possible, for yourself. Space on a plane is very limited, and spilled drinks are common.

When staying with friends or relatives, remember:

- Don't sweat the small stuff! Some routines may be hard to maintain, but if you are relaxed, the children will be, too.

- Small children who are trying to keep up with older children may need extra naps.

- Take your toolbox of skills with you, and pull out your bedtime routine. Keep bedtimes on schedule whenever possible. We all know that a tired child who goes to bed late does not sleep in!

- Take your family off for an afternoon or day trip every few days, just to give yourselves and your hosts a break.

- Pack easy wash-and-wear outfits. Don't worry if they wear T-shirts with a few ice cream stains. Remember, you are on holiday. Relax.

- Take your family rules with you. Even in a different household, basic family rules can be useful.

33 Family Times

I'm often asked how to help children develop good sportsmanship and the ability to be a team member. These are important life skills that will always be useful. One of the best places to learn sportsmanship and team playing is within the home team – the family.

Toolbox Skill

To promote family togetherness, establish dedicated time for family walks and games while children are young.

When two of my children became adults, I asked them how they felt they had learned these skills. They both agreed they had learned them when we did activities together like our family walks and family games. I could not believe what I was hearing. These were the same children who had to be dragged out for a walk, and invariably ended family games with one of them storming off in a huff because "the game sucked!"

If you try to make a habit of family time when the children are young, it then becomes part of the weekly routine. With all the fancy computer and video games available now, it is increasingly difficult to engineer family time. For family games, I recommend a set time every week, so the whole family knows that's the designated time to get together. We took turns selecting a game, which seemed to work well. Once our children were teens, I'd overhear them moaning to their friends on the phone that they couldn't go out because they had "a stupid family night tonight." I noticed, though, that they were always willing to participate when the time came. Maybe these "stupid family nights" provided an excuse to stay home and have some quality family time, but without losing face with their friends. Frequently, family games were exercises in patience, as the children experienced the art of winning and losing. Now, as adults, they assure me that this was all good experience. They realize what a lot they learned about themselves and each other, including how to play fair, to win and lose gracefully, and how to interact with others.

We started family walks when the children were quite small. Our walks were often long, and I discovered that little treats along the way were a huge incentive. I would also make up and tell stories to keep everyone plodding along without whining. It's amazing just how far a little one can walk, when engrossed in a story. Walks are valuable for school-age children as an opportunity for them to have some one-on-one time with a parent, and to be able to enjoy a conversation, uninterrupted by telephones and doorbells. Everyone is getting some exercise and, occasionally, something important is shared at these times. For teens, the act of walking side by side avoids those face-to-face confrontations they dread, and creates opportunities for parents to tackle difficult or touchy issues. Many times, I've been surprised by how much my teens have shared with me while we've walked together. We can all benefit from quality time spent as a family.

34 Bathroom Talk

Why is it that so many school-age children take such delight in babbling inanely about body parts and bodily functions? Children burst into giggles as they indulge in this silliness, and it can drive parents crazy.

Toolbox Skill

The place for bathroom talk is in the bathroom.

First, acknowledge and accept the existence of silly chatter about bathroom habits or body functions, because it won't go away until they outgrow it. Trying to force children not to talk that way just increases their delight in doing it. Once parents acknowledge and accept this irritating stage, they have taken a huge step towards saving their sanity. Second, allow bathroom talk, but not where it can drive you crazy. Location is the key. When children start with the bathroom nonsense, tell them, "I really dislike that kind of talk. If you need to use those words, please go to the bathroom, shut the door, and finish your chatter in there." At first, children find it quite novel to have permission to use these frowned-upon words. After a while, bathrooms become boring and the lack of an audience even more boring, and the novelty wears off. The best part for parents is that they no longer have to listen to it.

If bathroom talk happens in the car and one warning doesn't stop it, pull over whenever possible. Let the children know that it is not possible for you to drive while listening to that kind of talk. Ask them to let you know when they have finished, and ignore them until they stop. The thrill of using these naughty words often disappears when they no longer get the desired reactions from us.

35 Taking Responsibility

Toolbox Skill

Teach responsibility to children by demonstrating how to be organized yourself. Increase their levels of responsibility as children get older.

Whenever I work with parents of school-age children, the issue of responsibility seems to be their greatest concern. Parents experience huge frustration when their children dawdle, or don't do what they have been asked to do. We all want our children to be organized and responsible, because as adults we know life runs more smoothly that way. Responsibility has two parts to it. The child's part is to learn how to become responsible, and the parent's part is to model and teach responsibility.

Children will learn how to take on responsibility under the guidance of the parent. As children grow older, their responsibilities will increase. A young child can be responsible for putting on his socks each day. When he is nine years old, his responsibilities will have increased to include putting his dirty socks in the laundry, and helping with the sorting and folding of the clean laundry. By the age of fourteen, he can be completely responsible for all his laundry needs. If he neglects the task and runs out of clean clothes, he will learn the consequence of ignoring his responsibility.

Dawdling children can be a real frustration for parents in a hurry. Yet sometimes our own scheduling is contributing to the problem. Most of us have tight deadlines, especially first thing in the morning. We would like it if our children would understand both the need to hurry and why our frustration soars when we fall behind schedule. It helps when we recognize that it's our own schedule that's driving the frustration, not the dawdling child. And, when children are rushed, they seem to dawdle even more. When someone is hurrying me because of their schedule, I know I don't like it one bit. When I feel pressured, it seems to slow me down. I drop things, can't find things, and dig in my heels. I resent being rushed, and I think children feel the same.

Your responsibility is to make sure you have allowed enough time for yourself, even if it means getting up a few minutes earlier than usual. Expecting children to pick up the slack when we are running late is like expecting everyone on the road to drive faster or get out of our way when we're late for work. Let your children know the agenda and what you need them to accomplish.

If dawdling is a chronic problem in the morning, you could discuss some ways they could be more efficient with their time. Older children, for example, could make part of their lunch the night before. Younger children could select their clothes for the next day before they go to bed.

Logical consequences will also help you if you have a dawdler. Insist the child goes to bed 15 minutes earlier each night until the situation improves. Alternatively, his alarm could be set 5 minutes earlier each morning until a routine is established that works for you both. Let him decide which option to try. These consequences place appropriate responsibility on the child, and allow you to stay calm. You might also have to let him experience the consequence of not finishing his breakfast rather than being late for school.

36 Homework

Toolbox Skill

Set limits around homework times and how involved you get in school projects. Involve the children in some of the decisions about when and how homework should take place.

The challenge of homework is another topic that is frequently mentioned by parents of school-age children. We all want our children to do well, and many of us get too involved with larger school projects or jump in to help with homework left till the last minute. The result of too much parental involvement is that our children either can't work well by themselves, or they don't even bother to try.

An assignment that had lots of parental input may receive an A, but what did the child learn about the subject or about researching a topic and organizing the information? Your child may benefit from a discussion with you about the project, but you need to let the student do the work.

The first priority for parents whose children are having trouble getting their homework done is to set some limits around homework times. Involve the child in some of the decisions about when homework is to be done, so that she feels some control over what is ultimately her responsibility. Using clear communication, say, "Homework needs to be done tonight. What works best for you, doing homework once you've had a snack and an hour of playtime, or doing it after supper?"

With our own children, we found it very helpful to set a time for homework that was a quiet time for the whole family. The length of time increased as the children got older, and they could always do more if they wished. If homework was finished before the end of the allotted time, the children were encouraged to use the rest of the time for review or reading. We implemented a no-TV rule in our house from Monday to Thursday for everyone, including the adults. At first there was a great protest, and we were labelled "the meanest parents in the world." But eventually they accepted our rules, and were more willing to play games or read with us once their homework was finished. It brought us closer as a family, and they now tell me that when the time comes, the same limits will be in place for our grandchildren. We also implemented a no-phone-calls rule during the quiet time. We had to field the calls initially, but their friends soon caught on and knew when it was all right to phone. My husband and I made our calls while they were studying, and they made their calls once homework time was over.

Once our children became teens, we were so glad we had implemented the no-calls rule during homework time. The phone never stops ringing for teenagers. By chance, we had stumbled across the idea while the children were still in elementary school, so it was well established once they were teenagers.

A friend of mine would join her son at the kitchen table to do her paper work while he did his homework. She was role modelling what she expected from him, and was available for his questions. Not all children would like that arrangement, but it worked well for him and was a great way to lend an ear or to provide any required help.

37 The Shabby Side

Toolbox Skill

Accept your child's shabby side. It means they love and trust you enough to show you how they're really feeling.

Do you have an old shirt that you would never throw out, tucked away at the back of your closet? I do. Mine is faded and worn, but is nevertheless a most precious possession. I wear it around the house when I'm doing my chores, and sometimes I wear it just because it is comfortable and familiar. It's what I wear when I just want to be myself and don't need to impress anyone. It's okay for my family to see me in that shirt, but I would never wear it out in public because it is too shabby.

Most of us have an internal "shabby" side. It is the part of us that we never let outsiders see. Just like the old shirt, our shabby side feels familiar. It only emerges with those we trust and love the most and who we know love us in return. Here's an example of how adults sometimes present their shabby side.

Imagine that you and your partner have a furious argument just before leaving for a dinner with friends. You both get in the car, seething and not speaking. The atmosphere is icy. Then you arrive at the friends' house and are ushered in. Instantly, both of you are transformed into social, pleasant people. No one would ever know what was really going on between you. At the end of the evening, you get back into the car to drive home. The icy atmosphere returns, and you drive home in silence. You would never let others see that anything was wrong.

We feel safe in the knowledge that the special people in our lives accept us unconditionally, and will always forgive us in the end. It is safe to show them our not so pleasant, less than mature, not fully reasonable side.

Just like us, our children have a shabby side, too. A child who has been away all day at school or daycare has been trying hard to present her pleasant, social side. She will have had many experiences during her day, some good and some not so good. She may have had a problem with another child, been frustrated with an activity that didn't go well, or she may just be tired, because behaving well all day is tiring work. This child will have held in many of these feelings because she didn't feel safe enough to

It's Not A Plot To Drive You Crazy

let them out with people who are outside her family. When she sees Mom or Dad appear, it will be a huge relief because now she can let go and feel safe, surrounded by unconditional love. The unpleasant behaviour that may result will be easier to take when we understand why it happens.

Often the parents of a child who has just started full-day school will tell me, "The teacher says she is doing fine and is settling in well, but when I pick her up at the end of the day, she is rude and unpleasant with me." It makes sense to them when I explain about the shabby side. Their child has been trying so hard to fit in all day that she is now exhausted. Even though her behaviour would seem to indicate quite the opposite, she is telling them that she loves them best in the whole wide world and now feels safe to let her troubled feelings out. Teachers who listen to my talks will often nod their heads in agreement with this description. They know how hard school-age children try each day to meet the expectations school places on them. It's important for us to realize that the child's unpleasantness may not be directed at us and to encourage the child to talk about what has gone on. "It seems that you've had a difficult day. Do you want to tell me what happened?"

38 Life is Difficult

Life is a journey fraught with unexpected twists and turns. A large part of the growing-up process is discovering how to deal with the obstacles and hardships that crop up. With sensible guidance from parents and clear expectations of how to take on responsibilities, children should be well equipped to handle most of life's difficulties. But for some peculiar reason, many parents try desperately to shield their children from any hardships or difficulties.

Toolbox Skill

Help children to develop courage to face the challenges that life will present.

When we always rescue our children from distress, we are not helping them to develop the tools they will need to survive life without us. They need to develop courage and skill in order to face hardships and accept their limitations. Our job is to support and guide them so they can overcome some difficulties and to accept them for who they are.

A young child struggling to build a tower with blocks may become frustrated when his tower falls down. It would be easy for us to solve the problem by building the tower back up again. Instead, we need to encourage the child's attempts to keep trying, and celebrate his successes along the way. Parents of school-age children will sometimes interfere in solving an argument between their child and a school friend. This sends a message to the child that his parents don't have confidence that he can solve his own disagree-ment. He may need some guidance in effective communication skills, but what he most needs is his parents' belief in his ability to sort it out himself.

A teen who is angry because he didn't make the basketball team has a tough choice to make. He can focus his anger on the "stupid coach," or decide to practise harder so that he makes the team next year. His parents cannot protect him from his disappointment, but they can support him if he decides to work harder at his game, perhaps by arranging some extra coaching for him.

When children experience and survive life's adversities, they develop resilience and courage to face the many challenges that will come later. The hard part for parents is discerning when to stand back and support and when to leap in and protect their child. If you feel strongly that your child is in a situation that he is not mature enough to handle, then your gut instinct is probably right and he needs your help. Even at those more difficult times we can help children to break down the problem into smaller pieces and work with them, rather than taking over completely.

Recently I had a distress call from a friend whose seventeen-year-old daughter had suddenly announced plans to go off on a holiday with her boyfriend. My friend and her husband were united in their reaction to this announcement. They felt she was too young, and they just did not feel comfortable with it. When they refused to give their permission, tears and ranting from their daughter were the predictable result. My friend asked if I thought she was a terrible parent for causing her daughter such distress. My reply was, "Quite the opposite. I think you are excellent parents who have clear and reasonable rules and limits."

"But she is so upset," replied my friend. "She has shut herself in her room and won't speak to us." Their actions had made life difficult not only for their daughter, but for them, too. And sometimes that is one of the consequences of good parenting.

An important part of the growing-up process for children is learning that what they want may not be right for them at that particular time. That's why they still have parents to guide them along the way. Children learn that they can survive disappointments.

So what was the end result of my friend's dilemma? My friend spent a sleepless night thinking her daughter would never speak to her again, but the next morning her daughter appeared for breakfast, looking fresh and happy. The boyfriend's parents had also refused permission, so the two of them had decided the holiday plan was no longer an issue. Oh, the joys of being a parent.

PART 3

Tools For Talking And Listening

39

Alternatives to *No* and *Don't*

Toolbox Skill

Find alternatives to the words no *and* don't *whenever possible.*

The words *no* and *don't* may be the most frequently used words in a parent's vocabulary. We think saying *no*, or *don't*, will stop a child from doing something we don't like. When the child doesn't respond to the first *no*, many parents will repeat it, often adding, "*Don't*! I said *no*! *Don't* do that." Children soon learn that their parents will say the *no* word many, many times before they need to stop the offending behaviour.

While in a stationery store one day, I saw a couple chatting to one of the store clerks while their little girl, obviously bored, looked around and spotted a ladder leaning against the wall. She went over to it, and began to climb the first few rungs. Her father, seeing what she was doing, said, "*No*, Justine. Get down from there." Justine got down, and stared up at the ladder. Then her curiosity got the better of her, and she started to climb again. This time, her mother called out, "*No*, Justine. That's dangerous." Justine came down one rung, and waited for Mom to go back to her conversation with the clerk, before climbing up the ladder again. She sensed that her parents were not going to take any immediate action to stop her. After another *no* and *don't*, Justine's father came over to the ladder, lifted his daughter off and said, "Justine, get down. How many times have we told you not to do that?" Justine had learned that her parents would use the word *no* many times before she had to stop what she was doing. Dad or Mom could have taken action the first time she climbed the ladder by removing her, saying, "This is dangerous. Let's find something safer for you to do, while we finish our business."

I often ask parents to count the number of times in a typical day that they say *no* or *don't* to their children. The result of this exercise is to create a new awareness of how ineffective both words become when used too frequently. Once we are aware, we can explore alternatives to these words. There are better ways to establish good communication that include giving the child a clear reason for the parent's decision, and that allow the parent to be firm without inviting confrontation. Some alternatives to *no* might be:

Giving Information
Child: "Can I see if Matt can play?"
Parent: "Well, we're just about to have dinner, so I'm sorry but this is not a good time."

Here the parent is leaving out the words, "*No*, you can't," and instead gives information that will help the child to realize why this is not a good time to play with Matt.

Accepting Feelings

Child: "I don't want to go home now. Please, can we stay?"

Parent: "We do have to go home now. I know it's hard to leave when you're having fun."

Instead of, "*No*, we must go home," this parent is firm in his decision about leaving, but also shows empathy for the child's feelings. You're less resistant when someone understands how you feel.

Describing the Problem

Child: "Can we go to Auntie May's now?"

Parent: "We'll go as soon as I've finished folding the laundry. How about giving me a hand, and then I'll be finished even sooner?"

Rather than saying, "*No*, I'm not ready yet," this parent has clearly described her time constraints, and is inviting the child to participate in speeding up the process.

Substituting *yes* for *no*

Child: "Can I have some ice cream?"

Parent: "*Yes*, we'll buy some this afternoon when we go to the store."

It would have been easy for this parent to reply, "*No*. We don't have any." It is surprising how many times *no* can become *yes*.

These alternatives will take more time and thought than using the word *no*. But they get easier with practice, and they avoid the power struggles that are often created when we automatically just say *no*. If we have said *no*, but the child's persistence wears us down so that *no* changes to *yes*, then we have entered dangerous territory. Children are always prepared for a battle with the word *no*. Once we have shown them our minds can be changed, they will fight even harder to change every *no* to a *yes*.

There will be times when our answer is simply *no*, and that's all there is to it. Some issues may be just too complicated to explain to a child. But if we have made the effort to reduce our use of the word *no*, the child will realize this is one of those times when it is not wise to argue with our decision.

In times of danger, or to prevent an accident, parents will still need to use the words *no* or *don't*. If a child has not been fed a steady diet of these words, they are more likely to listen and to notice the urgency in the parent's tone of voice.

40 The Words *But* and *Why*

Toolbox Skill

Eliminate but *and* why *from your parenting vocabulary whenever possible. Encourage children to develop their reasoning powers from their why questions.*

The words *but* and *why* also cause difficulties in our parenting vocabulary. *But* is often used in the middle of a sentence and may negate the positive part of your message. The child only hears the words that follow *but.* "You combed your hair, *but* the back still looks messy." The word *why* is often used by a parent in such questions as, "*Why* did you do that?" This backs the child into a corner to find a reason that will appease the parent. Then there is the child's use of *why* questions, which can drive even the calmest parent insane. First, let's look at the problems with *but.*

A young child proudly shows you that he has dressed himself. You might say, "Look at you, all dressed and ready to go, *but* your shoes are on the wrong feet." The *but* diminishes the first part of the child's accomplishment. So a better comment would be, "Look at you, all dressed and ready to go." Eventually, he might feel the discomfort caused by the shoes, so wait a while. If nothing changes and you really can't stand it, you could add, "I wonder if your shoes feel comfortable like that?" If you comment on his error, the child may feel like a failure because he put his shoes on incorrectly. If you comment on his success alone, the child can enjoy the accomplishment of dressing.

A school-age child shows you some finished homework. You comment, "What neat writing, *but* why are your margins so wide?" This child may feel criticized and will only focus on the wide margins. Instead you could say, "What neat writing. There is lots of room in the margins. Did your teacher suggest that?"

A teenager seeks your opinion on a new shirt. You say, "I like the colour, *but* I don't think it will go with many of your things." A better comment would be to leave out the last part and simply say, "I like the colour."

The word *but* can have the same effect on adults. Imagine hearing, "Thanks for drying the dishes, *but* I wish you had put them away." You'd feel unappreciated and may think, "Nothing I do is ever good enough."

Now let's examine how the word *why* can become the other potential troublemaker. Whenever we ask children *why* they did something, the reply is inevitably, "Because," or "I don't know." Both those answers stop the dialogue we may be hoping to have. Eliminate the word *why* whenever possible and replace it with some of the other question words such as *how, what, where,* and *when.* Asking "What happened?" instead of "Why did you do that?" gives the child some room for an explanation. A question that starts with the word *why* boxes children in and forces them to justify their action. Young children often act impulsively, and honestly don't know why they did what they did, so how can they explain that to their parent? When a parent continues to say, "But why did you do that? I just want to know why," the child will stick to "Because" or "I don't know," which drives most parents to distraction. It's not a plot to drive you crazy. Try using the other question words.

When I talk to parents about their use of the word *why*, they often turn the tables and ask how they can survive the constant use of *why* by their children. It is an enormous task for children to sort and classify the myriad experiences and information that they absorb each day from their environment. Their minds are like sponges, constantly saturated by new knowledge. The *why* questions are their way of sorting information into the correct slot in their memory banks, not an attempt to drive a parent over the edge! But just because we understand why doesn't stop *why*, and parents still ask for some sort of respite from this barrage.

Sometimes parenting is like table tennis. The child bats the *why* to the parent, and the parent can bat it back to the child.

Child: "Dad, *why* do cats have fur?"
Dad: "Hmm, good question. *What* do you think?"

It's Not A Plot To Drive You Crazy

Rather than giving the child an immediate answer, Dad can use this opportunity to find out what the child knows about the subject. Encouraging the child to think for herself, rather than looking to Dad for a quick answer, will reduce many of the unnecessary *why* questions. Batting the question back will help to develop her reasoning powers. Of course, some questions do need a response, because the child genuinely may not have the knowledge. The role of a parent can be arduous, but it helps to remember that knowledge leads to independence, and independence gives the child the ability to leave home one day!

41 The Art of Buying Time

Toolbox Skill

Buy time. It costs nothing!

One of the tools I have found valuable on many occasions is knowing when to buy time. For some reason, we often feel we must have an instant answer to children's questions, or an immediate response to their misbehaviour. When we are uncertain about how to react to a child, the art of buying time can be very useful. When we are preoccupied or we lack energy, children have an uncanny knack of either asking for things or behaving badly. Maybe this is because at those times they sense there is a better chance that they'll get what they want. We may find ourselves reacting too quickly, or making snap decisions we later regret. If we had taken more time to think, we might have made a wiser decision.

Child: "Hey Mom, can Jason come over to play?"
Mom: "Not just now, I've got too much to do."
Child (beginning to pout): "But I'm bored and I've got nothing to do."
Mom: "I said no, and that's the end of it."

The child stomps off angrily and Mom begins to rethink the situation. She realizes that if Jason came over, the children would probably play well together and she could get her jobs done. But what can Mom do? If she changes her mind, is she being inconsistent and wishy-washy? Will the child think he can always get Mom to change her mind whenever he gets mad?

You can avoid some tricky situations by buying time. It's perfectly reasonable to take a little time before you react. If we get into the habit of responding to a child with, "Hmm, that's something I need to think about," we may avoid making a hasty decision and having to change our minds. Children of all ages feel respected when a parent gives full consideration to their requests, and even when the answer is not what they want, they may accept it more graciously because they know their parent gave it some careful thought. Buying time also gives a parent the opportunity to make a wiser decision, by exploring different options and seeking advice from other parents or parenting experts.

Allowing ourselves time to consider requests is an invaluable skill, especially as children get older. When we are asked about sleepovers by school-age children or about going to a party by a teenager, we will be glad to have the handy tool of buying time, so that we can give careful consideration to those requests. Older children can wait for answers longer than younger children, but they do need to have some idea of when a decision will be made. "Let me sleep on it and I'll have an answer for you by lunchtime tomorrow."

42 Using Fewer Words

Words can be useful tools. But if we use too many of them, our children may tune us out. For some peculiar reason, even when we've noticed they are not listening anymore, we often keep on speaking. Perhaps we think that by repeating the point, our message will eventually be understood. It doesn't usually happen!

Most of us dislike being lectured to, and children are no exception. Using a few words with a clear meaning has greater impact than a steady stream of explanations. A child hearing, "It's time for dinner. Please set the table," will be more willing to cooperate than if he hears, "How come I have to ask you every night to set the table when you know perfectly well it needs to be done. I don't know why I bother to prepare a meal because no one does anything to help around here…." All that the child hears after the first few words is, "Blah, blah, blah."

A clear, brief message also works best for little ones who are still mastering their language skills. "Time to brush teeth" or "Coats go on the hook" are simple directions that children can hear and follow easily.

Using fewer words with teens can encourage them to communicate more. Teens dislike being interrupted or judged by a parent, and will close down the communication quite quickly if the parent has too much to say or offers too much advice. When one of my teens wanted to talk, I found that, unless asked for a comment, it was best to listen before attempting to give a reply.

43

Listening

Toolbox Skill

*Listen attentively to
your children, so
that they learn how
to listen to you.*

Many parents complain that their children don't listen to them. "Whenever I try to talk to my daughter, she turns her head away and won't listen. How can I get her to pay attention to me when I need to tell her something?" Most of these parents have explored the possibility of the child having a physical hearing problem, and have come to the conclusion that their child hears what she wants to hear. They tell me that when topics such as favourite foods, an outing, or TV are mentioned, then the child has no difficulty hearing.

If I ask parents to think of the times when they know they don't listen well to their children, those times are immediately identifiable. When they're driving in the car, making dinner, folding laundry, or talking to a child from a different room, they're often too preoccupied to listen fully to their child. It's very understandable that parents don't always have time to listen attentively, but children need their parents to demonstrate good listening skills in order for them to acquire the ability to listen in return.

It would not be wise to suggest that every time a child begins to talk we drop everything to listen respectfully. Parents have busy lives, and children must learn that sometimes they may have to wait for a little while. How we communicate that message to them is very important. "I know you have something important to tell me and I'm looking forward to hearing what you have to say. I just have to put away these groceries first. If you help me, I'll be finished even sooner." This sort of communication validates that what they are trying to say is important to us. Since they do like to have our full attention, they are more likely to have a little patience. Once your task is completed, don't forget to follow through and listen to what your child wants to tell you.

Listening to children can be tiresome or inconvenient for parents at times. Sometimes teens will start an important conversation just as their exhausted parents are heading off to bed. We may need to suggest making time to talk with them in the morning. Many school-age children are brilliant at procrastination. They love to bring up all sorts of topics just when it's time for chores or homework. We could promise to set aside time to talk after homework or chores have been done.

When we role model attentive listening, children will absorb the skill as well. The child who refuses to listen and turns her head away needs guidance on how to listen. "I have something important to tell you. Finish putting that piece in your puzzle, then I need you to look at me and listen to me." When they have listened, be sure to say, "Thank you for listening so well. Now I know you have heard me and that you know what to do."

44 Eye Contact

We use eye contact to see whether someone is listening to us, and to show that person that we are listening, too. A few helpful points about eye contact that parents have shared with me include:

- Use eye contact for good news as well as bad. Sometimes we only insist on eye contact when a child is in trouble. Not surprisingly, children soon catch on, and will do anything to avoid looking at the parent, for fear of what is coming next.

- Some children really are uncomfortable with eye contact and with communicating face to face. Doing something together, like working on a puzzle or going for a walk, can be just as effective for talking and listening. The car is a good place for chatting, too.

45 The Balance of Power

Differences in power balance can cause awkwardness. Talking to a very tall person for a long time can cause a stiff neck. Towering over a very short person can leave you feeling slightly uncomfortable or awkward. We often speak to our children from high above them. If we want to establish good communication skills, it's a good idea to go down to their level, or to raise them up to ours.

It's Not A Plot To Drive You Crazy

When my children were little and we wanted to talk, I would put them up onto the kitchen counter or squat down beside them. They seemed to listen better when we could establish eye-to-eye contact. One father in a parenting group told us the following story, after we had talked about the benefits of eye-to-eye contact.

"After our discussion on power balance, I realized I was guilty of not coming down to my four-year-old son's level when discussing something with him. So the next time we talked, I made a point of squatting down in order to equalize our power balance. He looked at me in amazement, and promptly lay flat on the floor, so that he could be lower than I was!"

When the father realized that his son was so used to being "talked down to" and what this indicated about the difference in power, he made a special effort to equalize that balance from then on. Soon Dad and his son were able to chat eye-to-eye quite happily.

46 Talking

When my son Mike was about three years old, he developed a habit of blaming me for everything that happened to him. If he fell over and I was in the next room, I would hear him say, "Mom, look what you made me do!"

We, too, use blaming statements with our children. We say, "You are making me mad," when, in fact, we get mad all by ourselves. The child is not responsible for our feelings, and we need to take ownership for our feelings and responses by using "I" messages. An "I" message clearly states our feelings and makes us responsible for them, rather than putting the blame on the other person. "I'm angry because no one will listen to me" is more honest than "You never listen to me." When we use statements that blame, the receiver naturally becomes defensive and feels resentful. "Your room is always such a mess" may evoke the response, "No, it isn't. I cleaned it last week." Instead, the parent could say, "I'd like you to clean your room because the mess is bothering me." Using "I" statements won't necessarily mean the child will like what you say, but the message is clearer and less accusatory.

When children use blaming words, we can help them to rephrase their statement so that they, too, learn to take responsibility for their message. If you've insisted the TV be turned off and your child angrily responds with, "You're mean," your reply could be, "I think you are saying when I turn off the TV you don't like it."

My children used to warn their teenage friends that I would try to teach them to use "I" messages. It's a bit of a joke, but in fact my children do use them because "I" statements work to get the message across.

Wouldn't it be wonderful if communication skills were regularly taught in high school? Since good communication skills are important when teenagers are forming healthy, meaningful relationships, and are a basic requirement for most jobs, our teens would be developing an important life skill.

47 The Dangers of Using *Okay*

Toolbox Skill

Keep messages clear by leaving out okay.

While in the park the other day, I heard a parent say to her child, "Let's go home. Okay?" What could have been a very clear message – It's time to go home – was complicated by adding that one simple word – *Okay*. Using the word *okay* at the end of a statement can imply the child has a choice, even when the parent doesn't intend there to be one.

A young child might be told, "Put your shoes on, *okay*?" The parent wants the child to put his shoes on, so needs to state clearly, "Time to put your shoes on." A school-age child hearing the message, "Please clean up your room, *okay*?" may think the cleanup doesn't need to happen unless she feels like doing it. For most of these kind of statements, the action you as a parent expect is not optional.

A teen who is told, "No one is to sleep over while we are away, *okay*?" will likely be on the phone planning the first sleepover before the parents have left the driveway, because the message implied he had a choice.

In order to have our messages clearly understood by children, we must be sure not to create the possibility of an option when we do not intend there to be one. Using *okay* at the end of our sentences is confusing for children, and adds stress to parents' daily lives.

48 Writing Special Notes

Toolbox Skill

Once in a while, share your thoughts with your child using a written message instead of spoken words.

Another effective method of communicating with children, no matter what their age, is the written word. Written notes can describe what needs to be done, without the verbal wrangling, and it helps if you include a touch of humour, too. Written messages may also be useful for topics that children find sensitive or awkward to discuss in a face-to-face confrontation with a parent. The child can read the parent's written thoughts, and then has time to contemplate them before the parent and child sit down together.

Here's an example of a note written to my fourteen-year-old son in the hope it would motivate him to tidy his room:

"Hi, Mike. I am Henry, your bedroom. I'm glad you share my space, but I'm feeling a bit smothered by all the clutter in here. I'd breathe more easily if you created a bit of space for me. Signed, your bedroom buddy, Henry."

Mike never mentioned the note but the room did get tidied, and that prompted another note.

"Hey Mike, thanks! I love all the new space you've created. Signed, Henry."

Notes can be wonderful self-esteem boosters, too. When a child has achieved a success or fulfilled an obligation, a written word of thanks, affection or appreciation from a parent is both tangible and precious. The child has something real to remind him of his accomplishment.

A note tucked into a lunchbox that says, "Hi, I love you," will bring a smile to a child's face and may give him a lift to help him through his day. It takes only a minute to write a few words, but the encouragement for the child is huge. Even little ones who are unable to read are thrilled to receive a note, and will ask you to read it to them many, many times.

49

The Phone

The phone is an instrument used for communication, and is also a source of annoyance for parents. I see many parents roll their eyes when the phone is mentioned. It seems to be common that when parents are on the phone, the children start to act up and demand attention. They may have been happily occupied, but the minute the phone rings or a parent tries to make a call, suddenly they are desperate for parents' attention.

Toolbox Skill

Carefully choose your timing for making phone calls. When calls come in, be prepared to delay the call until a more convenient time.

Older children may also take advantage of our phone times. When we are on the phone, they know we are not giving them our undivided attention and there's always the possibility they could slip something by us. When I was engrossed in phone conversations, my teenage son became adept at making announcements like, "Hey, Mom. I'm just borrowing your car for a while, okay?" He knew it was easier for me to agree than to get off the phone and discuss his request.

I had often wondered why the phone seems to have such a negative impact on children. Then, one day, as I was standing in a store lineup waiting to pay the cashier, I realized that the phone is an unwanted and unexpected interruption for children. The phone at the cashier's till rang and she picked it up. Instantly, her attention was focused on the caller, and she was no longer serving those of us who were still waiting patiently in the line. It is the same for children. They may be happily playing, but they know that we are at hand and available should they need something. When the phone rings and we answer it, they know we are no longer available. When children sense that our attention is elsewhere, they will try to get the focus back on them. The best way to achieve that is to do something we won't like, because then we'll definitely notice them.

There are some ways we can alleviate some of the challenges caused by the phone. If you have calls to make, try to pick a time of day when your child is happy to play on her own. Make sure you spend some time with her before you make your calls, perhaps playing or reading with her. Some parents find it useful to let young children have a toy phone, so that they can also phone their friends while you make your calls. One parent told me she and her son made a list of all the calls they had to make, and then crossed them off as each call was completed. He enjoyed crossing off the names, and it gave him a clear idea of how long Mom's calls would take.

Use your tools of communicating clearly and involving the child in choices. "I need to make three phone calls. You may play quietly with your blocks in here with me, or you can play in your room – you decide." If the child chooses to stay with you but will not be quiet, help her to her room and remind her that by her actions, she has chosen to play there while you finish your calls. It may take a while for a young child to understand that she made the choice to leave, so be sure to follow through consistently.

It's often more difficult for you and for your child when you receive phone calls that you hadn't expected. If it's the wrong time and you know you won't be able to have a reasonable conversation, then ask the caller if you can get back to them. If the call is important but your child needs you, try using the mute or pause button if your phone has one, so the caller can't hear your conversation with your child. That gives you a chance to listen to your child, rather than agreeing to something you might later regret. It also provides you with a few moments to help the child choose an activity, or to remove her to a safe place while you finish the call.

If we allow it, the phone can easily dominate us and interrupt our lives. When talking to your children, having a meal, or during family time, let the answering machine take the calls. This shows respect for your family members.

50 Teenage Flashes of Adult Logic

On occasion, because teens are adult-sized, parents fall into the trap of expecting them to think and behave like adults. Teens still have parents around because they're not yet ready to consistently make adult decisions. Teens still need parents to provide direction and guidance, even though they may not think they do!

Toolbox Skill

Teenagers still need limits, even when they show flashes of responsible adult thinking. Don't be fooled. Stay alert!

Studies show that the teenage brain is not fully developed in the areas of reason and logic until about the age of eighteen or nineteen. These studies reassured me that I still had a parenting role to fulfill with my teens, and helped me to continue to be firm and consistent with setting limits. Occasionally, parents will notice a flash of adult reasoning and logic from a teen. These flashes may deceive the parents into thinking their teen is now fully mature. Not so! I believe the flashes can give parents hope that the mature adult is emerging slowly, but surely, from the childhood cocoon. These brief periods of adult logic are not necessarily sustainable, and it is important not to be lulled into false expectations. This is just a part of normal teen development.

51 Arguing with Teenagers

Arguing with teens can be even more exhausting than arguing with little ones. Teens have well developed debating skills, as well as the time to whittle away a parent's resolve. There are some common techniques that are useful when entering into discussions with teenagers.

Teenagers can be masters at knowing how to trigger our anger when they argue with us. I have found that when I am angry, I often come down to the level of my teenager and the battle for supremacy is on. It is crucial that we remember we are the adults and that we behave accordingly. It works best if we can deliver our messages succinctly and, if possible, without anger. You may need to find ways to calm yourself before entering into the discussion.

If tempers start to flare, it is excellent role modelling to walk away, saying, "Let's end our discussion for the time being, and cool off. How about talking again this afternoon, when we've both had some time to think?" As you turn to walk away, try as hard as you can to ignore the parting shot that the teen may fire at you. Often this is a swear word or a nasty comment. Recognize that it is designed to stop you in your tracks and embroil you in the fight again, so let it go. Later on, when things are calmer, remind them that bad language is unacceptable, and that you expect to be treated with the same respect you give to them.

Be sure that when you lose your temper, and even the most patient of parents will, you offer a genuine apology. "I'm sorry I lost my temper this morning, and I'd like to try to talk again. Is that agreeable to you?" Remember not to put a *but* in your apology, as in "I'm really sorry I was so angry, but you frustrate me at times," as this will just escalate the argument, and is not a full apology.

It's Not A Plot To Drive You Crazy

52

Saying Sorry

"How do I get my child to say she's sorry when she has done something wrong?" This question frequently arises among parents.

If our child has hit or shoved another child, we may feel embarrassed, and surprised that she would act that way. If the victim is weeping and wailing and causing a lot of attention to be drawn to the situation, we may worry that other adults will view us as bad parents. Out of embarrassment, we then react by scolding our child and trying to force an apology, although really we have two goals. We want to appease the other adults to reduce our own embarrassment, and we also want our child to make an attempt to right the wrong that has happened.

Demanding apologies from children can create some difficulties. Parents are not always aware of the real story. It may be that the victim provoked the attack. Forcing children to say they're sorry teaches them that simply saying those words can get them out of trouble. They quickly learn the words do not need to be sincere. A forced apology is seldom genuine. If we revisit our goals of wanting our children to become responsible and accountable, then surely a forced apology is counterproductive. Still, we are left with the dilemma of how to help our child make reparations.

If we know that our child is definitely the culprit, we can focus on the hurt child, making sure attention goes to him. We can role model an apology. "Tom, I'm sorry you got hurt and I hope you'll feel better soon." Most parents of the innocent child are very understanding. Many of them will have experienced their child being the aggressor at some time or other. If you don't know for sure who the culprit was, it is best to leave apologies out and suggest the children play separately for a while.

Be sure to demonstrate genuine apologies in your own home. Make sure children see or hear you apologize to your partner or other family members. Many times if I've overreacted with my children, I've apologized after I've calmed down by saying, "Nick, I lost it this morning and I'm very sorry. Can we make a fresh start?"

53 The Gift of Forgiveness

Forgiveness is a word we all know, but it can be quite a feat to be a forgiving person. We may find it challenging to wipe the slate clean and truly forgive someone, even when they have genuinely apologized.

Parents tend to remember their children's mistakes, long after the event. "I hope you will remember to put your swimsuit in your backpack after your lesson today, and not forget it like you did last week."

Children, on the other hand, are very forgiving. When I've made parenting mistakes, my children have been willing to forgive and forget. Younger children seldom hold a grudge and are almost always prepared to forgive their parents for the small, everyday mistakes they make. Sometimes our children can teach us a skill. We can learn a lot from our children when they display forgiveness and unconditional love.

PART 4

Tools For Disciplining With Love

54

Being Respectful

Most parents want their children to learn respect – to respect others, to be respected by others, and to respect themselves. You can't learn respect if you're not shown respect. So learning respect starts with the respect we as parents show to our children.

Toolbox Skill

Children who receive respect from their parents will learn to respect themselves and others.

In their first few years, children are learning how to belong in their world. All their experiences are new, and they learn both what is acceptable and what is not from their parents' reactions. Those reactions should be respectful, if children are to learn how to respect in return. But sometimes we do slip up.

Imagine you're having a family barbeque when one of your children drops a glass and it breaks. Even though you know it was an accident, you might react by saying, "Look what you've done! I've told you a hundred times to hold those glasses carefully." Now let's imagine that a few of your adult friends are over for a barbeque one evening, and one of the guests drops his glass. I'm sure you would be very gracious and say, "Please don't worry. It was just an accident, and those glasses are easily replaced." You would do your best to reduce the embarrassment your guest would be feeling.

Although these situations are not exactly parallel, in that you are not responsible for "raising" your guest, you likely would spend more effort reducing your guest's embarrassment than your child's. Sometimes we try to correct without being sensitive to the child's feelings, and that is not respectful. Children usually feel very bad when accidents happen. If you try to imagine how you would feel if you were the one who had broken the glass, it may help you to treat your child as respectfully as you would treat anyone else.

Another way we sometimes slip up is by not using a respectful tone of voice with our children. My children have told me, on occasion, not to use "that voice." I was not aware that I was using "that voice" until I listened to myself. Then I could hear my patronizing and belittling tone. "We hang our coats up in this house, not throw them in the corner." They were right, and had they used that tone with me, I would have felt disrespected, too.

When we show respect for our children, they will develop a clearer sense of their self-worth. Encouragement from us and the other influential adults in their lives gives them the courage to try new things, to enjoy successes, and to accept the inevitable failures. Positive reactions from us will help them to build confidence. If we give support to our older children without rescuing them when they must deal with a difficult situation, their self-respect will continue to grow. Letting them know that you believe they can handle a problem themselves will inspire them to try. Older children will also need your guidance to know which situations need the advice of an adult.

Showing respect to others comes more easily to children who have seen respect shown to them. They watch interactions between adults and absorb the components of healthy relationships. When parents make time to interact respectfully with their children, the children will learn how to respect others. They may need some help with how to respect the feelings of others. "I know you are really angry that Danny let you down. I think maybe he needs a friend right now. His parents are getting divorced, and perhaps he's having a hard time." Learning all the facets of respect takes time and effort, but eventually leads to healthy self-respect which we all want for our children.

55 Skills for All Ages

Some parenting skills work all the way through the child's journey to adulthood – clear communication, consistency, using choices, and appropriate consequences. Other tools, such as dealing with bathroom talk, are put away as children mature. But no matter what skills you use and for what length of time, they are based on respect for the child.

Some common parenting methods, however, work for the short term but are not respectful and not sustainable. One of those most frequently used is "counting" or time ultimatums. "I'm going to count to three, and then…." Counting seems to work some of the time when a child is small, but it's based on fear. The child is uncertain and a little fearful of what will happen when the parent reaches the number three.

There are other problems with counting, too. When I ask parents if they know what they will do once they reach three, most of them have no idea. They just hope the child will comply. I remember counting with my own children and getting to a ridiculous point where I resorted to using fractions. I, too, had no plan of what to do after reaching three, so I would say, "Two and a quarter, two and a half…." I needed to prolong the counting, hoping that the children would eventually obey. It doesn't take long for even young children to catch on to the parent's dilemma.

While visiting a friend of mine recently, I observed how using counting sometimes backfires for the parent. My friend, the mother of two-year-old Matt, was experiencing her son's discovery that he had a mind of his own. When my friend suggested we all walk to the park, Matt happily agreed. Mom asked Matt to put his shoes on, so that we could leave. Matt, distracted by a truck he'd discovered under the couch, ignored her request. Mom asked Matt, rather more firmly, to put on his shoes, but instead he picked up one shoe and threw it across the room. His mother, managing to stay calm, told him to fetch his shoe and put it on. Matt continued to play with the truck. Mom began to count, "That's one." No reaction from Matt.

It's Not A Plot To Drive You Crazy

"That's two." Nothing happened. "That's three," said Mom in exasperation, but even reaching three did not faze Matt, who was quite happy with his newly found truck. What could Mom do now?

We adults were all ready to go, but it was obvious Matt now had a different agenda and didn't care if we went or not. Counting had not worked, and Mom had no appropriate consequence in mind. Rather than using counting, Mom could have said, "Matt, we're going to the park now. You need your shoes on. Put them on yourself, or I will help you with them." If Matt had continued to ignore his mother, she could then have helped him with his shoes, confident that her communication had been clear and that he had made his choice.

Issuing a time ultimatum, such as counting, depends on fear to be effective and is not respectful of a child of any age. Using clear communication, choices, and having appropriate logical consequences will produce more cooperation over the long term of parenting.

56 The Lure of Curiosity

There are times when a child's curiosity can lead her to repeat behaviour that's led before to unpleasant results. It's almost as though the lure of curiosity overrides the memory of what happened the last time.

Toolbox Skill

Your calm, firm, and consistent reactions will appease your child's natural curiosity to test you.

When our son Mike was three, he was playing barefoot in the back garden. Despite my explanation that the bees hovering in the clover on the lawn might sting him if they were stepped on, he firmly planted his foot on a bee and was stung. Tears flowed, cuddles and soothing medication were administered, and after a while he felt better. I thought he had probably learned a valuable lesson, but to my amazement he went back to the same patch of lawn and used his other foot to purposefully step on another bee! His memory of the pain wasn't sufficient to diminish his curiosity. Would it happen again? He just had to know.

That same curiosity comes into play when children and parents interact. Parents often tell me they think their children do things over and over again that they know will deliberately annoy them. Such repetitive behaviour is bewildering. Surely this can't be fun for the child! When adults receive negative feedback, they try to avoid repeating the offending behaviour. So what's going on in children's minds? It is not surprising that parents think children do things to drive them crazy.

A little one will touch the controls on the TV, while grinning and watching the parent for a reaction. The child probably remembers that the last time he touched the TV controls, Dad got pretty angry. But the child's curiosity to test the consistency of Dad's reaction overrides that unpleasant memory.

The more the child touches the forbidden controls, the more annoyed Dad becomes. This fuels the child's curiosity because the intensity of Dad's reaction keeps changing. So the child repeats the behaviour, looking for consistency. What can be done to stop the cycle? It's most important that the parent's reaction be firm and consistent. Be concise with your words. "The TV is not a toy. Let's find your farm animals." Or quietly remove the child, redirecting him to another activity. Every time the child goes back to the TV, use the same consistent reaction and redirection. His curiosity about the consistency of your reaction may then be satisfied. By using the same approach every time, you can put a stop to many of the irritating behaviours.

57 Being Creative

Toolbox Skill

Try a little creativity to ease the frustrating times.

How can we avoid power struggles and the frustration that accompanies them? A bit of creative fun will often help. Most children respond to a sense of humour. Clothes that talk to a child go on more easily. A shoe could say, "Hi, Lisa. Hurry up and put me on, so we can go out to play." Your child could make a badge that reads, "I dressed myself!" Not only is this a fun activity, but may eliminate your embarrassment when she chooses unusual style or colour combinations. Singing or clapping a familiar song or rhyme can act as a distraction and avoid a public scene.

One mother told me how she used singing as a distraction. "The three of us were taking the bus home from gym class the other day. I carried the baby onto the bus while five-year-old Molly climbed on by herself after me. But she tripped on the bottom step and fell on her knees. When she burst into loud sobs, that scared the baby and he began to scream, too. A couple of people tried to help and found us seats. But my two still kept crying and I didn't know what to do. Everyone was looking at us. Then I remembered Fran's suggestion about singing, and over the noise I began to sing, 'The wheels on the bus go round and round….' A lady sitting across from me joined in, and soon several others were singing along, too. The children were so surprised that they stopped crying, and watched fascinated as all these grown-ups sang 'The Wheels on the Bus.' Now I keep a list of songs in my mind wherever I go."

Many parents sigh when I describe the tool of being creative. "It takes too much energy," they complain. Yes, being creative does take some thought and energy, but it's less tiring than an exhausting power struggle.

It's Not A Plot To Drive You Crazy

58 Dealing with Tantrums

Frustration is the root cause of most temper tantrums. Tantrums are common for young children aged eighteen months to four years, as they lack the language skills to express their frustrations to their parents. They also have a limited understanding of their own emotions. Older children may experience tantrums, too, when they feel extreme rage or frustration.

Tantrums fall into two categories, frustration tantrums and power tantrums. Frustration tantrums are the most common and are like erupting volcanoes. The child reaches a point where frustration overwhelms him. He loses control and is beyond any logic or reason. Small children often use their bodies to convey their lack of control. Some hit, while others throw themselves onto the floor and thrash around, screaming loudly. Older children may attack each other physically or verbally, or use foul language to indicate their loss of control. Yelling and door slamming often accompany their tantrums.

Power tantrums occur if a child gets what he wants after having a frustration tantrum. The child may now use tantrums as a tool. The volume and intensity of the tantrum may increase if the tantrum doesn't seem to be producing the desired result. After a while, some parents may notice that the child watches them to observe their response or uses forced sobbing, which is often indicative of a power tantrum.

If parents react by arguing with or yelling at a child who is out of control, the intensity of the tantrum will usually increase. Children experiencing tantrums are out of control. They don't need their parents to be out of control, too. Tantrums are frightening, and parents are the child's security.

With small children, it is imperative that the parents stay with them. But each child may need a different response. Some need to be held or rocked, some need to be left to thrash it out while the parent remains nearby, and some respond to soft humming. When the tantrum is over, try to continue on as if the tantrum had not happened. It's important for children to realize that throwing a tantrum will not achieve their objective, if they had one in mind. Later, some children will need to discuss what happened, and some will prefer to carry on as if nothing had happened. You will know what works best for you and your child. Each tantrum eventually ends, though a power tantrum may last for some time until the child realizes that the parent will not give in.

Older children often need a place where they can calm down and be alone, perhaps in their own room, the family room, or the den. What a great opportunity for parents to role model walking away from conflict that is out of control, while demonstrating effective communication skills. "Let's take a break from one another, and talk about this after supper when we've cooled down."

Prevention is key with tantrums. Here are some effective ways to avoid them:

- Before frustration overwhelms them, redirect small children away from activities that are too challenging. Show older children how to take a break from a difficult activity, returning to it later.

- Take care of children's basic needs. Hunger, fatigue, over-stimulation, and curiosity can all trigger tantrums.

- End activities while they are still going well. Even an enjoyable visit with a friend can end in disaster if the friend stays too long.

- Build stress-relievers into your child's day. Quiet time, reading, exercising, or listening to music can all help to reduce frustration levels.

- Offer choices, so children can experience a sense of control over their lives.

- Before an outing, inform children about what is going to happen and your expectations of their behaviour.

- If a tantrum should happen in public, behave exactly as you would at home, or remove the child as efficiently as possible to a more private location. Ignore comments from passersby, unless they are supportive.

- Keep an arsenal of activities, snacks, and toys for those unavoidable long waits.

- Remind yourself that tantrums are normal and do pass.

- Don't sweat the small stuff. Some battles are not worth fighting.

59 Two Invisible Attributes

Most parents see the benefits of noticing and acknowledging positive behaviour. But what can be done to prevent negative attention-seeking such as needless whining or arguing, behaviour that drives most parents mad?

Children are making discoveries about life by observing parental reactions to their behaviours. Even when our reactions are not pleasant, they still have our attention. For children, any form of attention is better than being ignored. Some careful thought about how children manage to engage their parents, using negative behaviour, led me to the conclusion that children have two invisible attributes.

The first is that children are masters of the art of arguing. They have a hidden debating and arguing degree, and a lot more time than their parents do to engage in lengthy debates about any issue, large or small. Unfortunately, their ability to argue is not matched by their ability to reason, so arguments with children are often fruitless. Trying to reason logically with them in the hopes that they will see our point of view can be exhausting.

The other invisible attribute is their ability to hook a parent into an argument and then reel them in. It's almost as if they have a hidden fishing rod that has juicy bait attached. The child is adept at dangling the bait in front of his unsuspecting parent, and waiting for him to bite. Whining is a perfect example of how a parent can be tempted to take the bait.

Whining often occurs around dinnertime, probably because most parents are busy preparing the meal and not paying attention to the child, who may be hungry. The child has discovered that whining triggers annoyance, which results in attention. Once the whining child has hooked the parent, all that's left is to reel him in. Either the child gets what he is whining for, or gets an argument. In both cases, the child has successfully gained some attention.

When we are aware of these two invisible attributes we can often find more positive ways such as redirection or distraction to deal with needless whining and arguing.

60 Surviving Negative Attention-Seeking

What does a parent do to avoid taking the bait and being hooked into a power struggle? With very small children, distraction or redirection to another activity works most of the time. Try bringing out some different toys or play dough that is kept aside for those difficult times. When I was busy in the kitchen, I encouraged my children to play with the pots and pans. This provided great distraction, and kept the children in the same room with me. Some parents play music for their little ones to dance to, or record a favourite story on tape to entertain them. Some parents pop young children into an early bath to change the mood. Small children can also help with preparing dinner, peeling or scrubbing vegetables with supervision. Older children who are hungry or bored can help to get dinner ready, too. Interestingly, they often find something to do very quickly after that suggestion!

Toolbox Skill

Distraction or redirection work well to divert negative attention-seeking. Identify the child's need behind a recurring pattern of misbehaviour.

If parents see their children's behaviour following a pattern day after day, that's a clue that it is time for a change of reaction or schedule. Children have low energy by late afternoon and are often fractious and difficult during that time. They are not mature enough to understand why they feel that way, so they let us know by trying to engage our attention. This is when the whining begins, and the fishing rod emerges. Perhaps the child is hungry, and a plate of raw vegetables will fill a void without spoiling dinner. Maybe the dinner hour is too late for the child and needs to be moved to an earlier time. Try to look for the child's need behind his behaviour. It's not a plot to drive you crazy. Use your inner resource of creativity to see if you can find a way to change both your pattern and his, and restore peace and harmony.

61 Strong-Willed Children

Parents often tell me that they are concerned because they have a very strong-willed child. I'm sure if we explored the backgrounds of many of our world leaders, their parents probably classified them as strong-willed children, too. We need strong-willed people in our world, but as children, they do present some challenges for their parents.

When I work with parents, one of the first questions I ask them is what they most want for their children. The responses are fairly uniform. They want their children to be happy, confident, respectful, independent, and socially acceptable, to name a few. I then suggest that these parents are forgetting something, because what we all really want is for our children to move out one day. This generates some laughter, but actually it is true. We want to equip our children with all the skills they need to be able to lead independent, healthy lives. It is interesting that when children first begin to display some of those desired traits, normally around the age of two, their parents rush in panic for parenting books and courses. Instead, parents should celebrate when they see the first sign of determined behaviour. Here it is, the first small step towards leaving the nest!

Despite recognizing that a strong will can be beneficial later in life, parents with determined children still find their behaviour challenging and tiring. One father was nearly out of his mind with frustration because his three-year-old daughter seemed obsessed with climbing to the top of the bookshelves in his home. Naturally he was worried she would fall, and he knew that she was not aware of how dangerous her actions were. He felt he had tried everything to stop her, including barricades, threats, and sending her to her room. Nothing worked. She was determined to climb to the top. That was her mission.

Patience and consistency are the key elements in dealing with determined children. Understanding the child's need behind the behaviour, and having a plan of action to satisfy the need in a less dangerous way, are also crucial. In this case, the father identified his daughter's strong desire to climb, and also realized she was getting attention from him every time she climbed the shelves. This was a double payoff.

To fix what he saw as a problem, Dad first prepared himself mentally to try to be calm and patient when responding to his daughter's behaviour. He formed a plan of action. Every time she headed towards the bookshelves, he would say, "Looks like you need some climbing time." Then he would take her outside to the garden where they had a climbing frame and would give her lots of attention while she climbed the frame. He was also able to enroll her in a gymnastics class for toddlers that included balancing activities. His consistency eventually paid off as the little girl responded to the positive attention she received when climbing in a safer place. After a while, the shelves no longer held such allure.

62 Looking for the Child's Need

Toolbox Skill

Before responding to an unwanted behaviour, step back and identify the child's need.

Sometimes we need to step back from a situation and explore it from a different perspective. Looking at concepts from a child's point of view can provide useful insight. Parents who take the time to examine what is going on for their child will have a much clearer idea of how to set appropriate limits. We often react instantly to unruly behaviour without taking a few seconds to understand what is motivating that behaviour.

A mother in one of my groups related the following story. Her ability to see things through the eyes of her child led her to understand better her child's need and come up with a creative solution.

"We live on the top two floors of a house and rent the downstairs suite to a tenant. Our four-year-old daughter loves to jump off the bottom three stairs over and over again. I try desperately to make her stop, because I know it must disturb the poor tenant to hear the constant thumping. Emma doesn't understand why I get so angry with her, but I can't afford to lose the tenant."

Mom had realized Emma could not understand why her jumping caused such trouble. Mom also recognized that the negative attention she was giving to the jumping was probably causing that behaviour to continue. What a dilemma, but Mom couldn't ignore the behaviour or she might lose her tenant. So we looked at it through Emma's eyes and tried to identify the child's need. A four year old has discovered how to jump and is perfecting her skill with enthusiasm. She needed an appropriate place that would allow her to master her skill without disturbing others. Once we had identified this basic need, Mom knew instantly what to do. She came up with the idea that her daughter could jump, but only when the tenant was at work. Together Mom and Emma drew up a schedule so that each day she knew when she could jump.

Many times we react to a child's behaviour with frustration because of our own agenda rather than looking for the child's need.

63 One Step Forward, Two Steps Back

Toolbox Skill

By accepting regressive behaviour without argument, we help the child to be able to let go of that behaviour and move on.

Once a child has mastered a skill, we assume that they've got it for life and will never lose it. But even though they may have acquired the skill, sometimes they just want someone else to do it for them. An example of this might be when a young child manages to dress himself for the first time. His parents are delighted and encouraging about the new achievement. Then, a week later, the child no longer wants to dress himself and says, "I can't do it. You do it for me."

The parent cajoles the child, saying, "Oh, sure, you can do it. You've been dressing yourself for a whole week now." There is a strong possibility that the child will then dig in even harder, because he wants to regress to being less capable and feeling little again. His parents worry that he will never dress himself again, and insist that he do it on his own. A power struggle may result, and start even more battles about getting dressed.

Let's look at this behaviour from an adult perspective. I know how to cook. In fact, I'm reasonably good at it. There are times, however, when I just don't feel like cooking, and want someone else to cook for me. This doesn't mean I'll never cook again. I just need someone else to take over, so I can have a break. It is the same with the child. He may feel overwhelmed by always being expected to dress himself, and just needs a break or some help from his Mom or Dad. How we react to this backwards step is crucial.

If we acknowledge his feelings and provide him with some cooperation, the problem may dissipate fairly quickly. If we try to force what we want, then a battle will ensue. Instead of trying to persuade him to get dressed, we could say something like, "I guess you don't feel like dressing yourself today. I can help you this time, but it sure will be great when you can dress yourself again. Now where's that sock?" The parent's acknowledgment of the child's feelings, and willingness to cooperate, may prevent the issue from escalating further. Every child wants to grow up, so we don't need to worry that he has regressed forever. If you're worried about regressive behaviour, it helps to look into the future and study some older children. All the teens I know dress themselves.

64 GUCK

Toolbox Skill

*Whenever you see
an opportunity to
relinquish some
control, use GUCK:
Giving Up Control
of Kids.*

If we constantly interfere in our children's lives, we send them a message that we don't believe they are capable. This undermines their self-confidence. Then we complain that they are not responsible enough. It's a constant juggling act as we struggle with situations that involve relinquishing control. We don't want a two year old to get hurt, so we never let her fall. We don't want a school-age child to fail, so we remind him over and over to bring his class project home. We don't want our teen to be late, so we drive her when she sleeps in.

So how do they learn what happens when they fall, forget a project, or sleep in? They don't, unless we provide safe opportunities for them to learn to be responsible. It's hard to stand by and watch your child learn a valuable lesson when you could so easily rescue them from pain and distress, but children need those experiences so they'll take control of their own lives one day.

I recommend to parents that they practise GUCK: Giving Up Control of Kids. Let's allow our children the freedom to make some of their own choices and learn from the consequences. Some of their decisions will be good ones and some will be learning experiences, but by allowing them to exercise some of the control for their lives, we will be helping them with their quest for independence.

A friend of mine was having a difficult time rousing her son in time for school. He liked school and didn't want to be late, but he'd crawl out of bed at the last minute. She would drive him to school to help him avoid being late, knowing he hadn't had any breakfast and probably hadn't even brushed his teeth. She was exasperated and asked me to help. "Use GUCK," I suggested. "Give up control of your kid." She pointed out that her son was already experiencing the consequences of bad breath and going without breakfast. "Yes," I agreed. "But he knows you'll rescue him by driving him if he's running late. So tell him you won't drive him unless he's ready by a certain time, with breakfast inside him and his teeth brushed, and stick to it." That evening, my friend explained her new expectations to her son, making sure he fully understood the arrangement. The school was within a reasonable walking distance, so she knew he could easily get there if he gave himself enough time. Next morning, he was not up at the designated time, so she busied herself on the computer and let events unfold.

He raced in as usual, about 5 minutes before school began, and said, "Hey, Mom. I'm ready to go."

It's Not A Plot To Drive You Crazy

She calmly replied, "We agreed that I'd drive you if you were ready to go by 8 o'clock, having had breakfast and with your teeth brushed. It is now 8:15, so you'll have to make your own way."

"Yeah, but just this once, help me out, Mom," he pleaded.

"Sorry," said Mom, "you're on your own this morning." He realized she was not budging, so with a flurry of activity, and swearing under his breath, he raced out the door. It took several days before he was convinced his mother was serious, but she remained steadfast and gave up control to him. Only when she stopped rescuing him was he able to take responsibility on his own.

65 Discipline or Punishment

Toolbox Skill

Use discipline to teach, rather than punishment.

We want our children to attain independence and become responsible, accountable human beings. As we look for ways to help them accomplish these goals, the topics of discipline and punishment invariably come up for discussion among parents. However, punishment and discipline are quite different concepts.

Punishment teaches children to avoid a behaviour out of fear of the parent's reaction. Discipline teaches them to avoid a behaviour because they have learned to anticipate the related consequence of that behaviour, and are then able to make a conscious choice about it. Discerning the difference between these two concepts can be tricky.

A child who takes and eats her brother's candy can learn a different lesson if her parent punishes her than if he disciplines her. If the child is punished by being yelled at and sent to her room, she will be more absorbed with her own resentment of the treatment she is receiving than with making amends to her brother. There's no related consequence between the actions of eating the candy and being sent to her room. Punishment tends to be about the parent controlling the child by making her fear the suffering that will be inflicted if she's caught. The parent wants to make sure the child never again repeats that behaviour. Because punishment is seldom related to the misbehaviour, the child may react by trying to find a way to avoid getting caught the next time, or by taking out her resentment on someone else, such as a younger sibling. Punishment certainly lets the child know she has done wrong, but there is generally no understanding of the real impact of her actions.

Discipline, on the other hand, comes from the Latin *disciplina* meaning teaching. If she's asked to use her allowance money to replace the brother's candy, she's taught that when she takes something that is not hers, her responsibility is to replace it. Discipline teaches children that there are consequences to their actions, so that they learn over time to weigh those consequences. Children will still do wrong at times, but the ability to think things through before acting will help them to make wiser decisions, especially during the times when there are no parents around.

Discipline relates the result to the act, so the child sees the impact of her actions on herself and others. Were someone else's rights or property harmed by her behaviour? If so, how can she put things right? If she told a lie, how will others trust her in the future and how can that trust be rebuilt? When we teach children through discipline to consider the impact of their choices, we encourage them to make better decisions and to develop respect for themselves and others.

A father told me the following story about his two sons, aged two and four. One Saturday, they went to visit the father's sister who needed help installing a computer program. The boys were allowed to bring their current favourite toy, a wooden train set. The two adults were soon engrossed in their work, while the boys played happily in the living room. The boys noticed a space between the couch and the wall and invented a new game. They would try to throw the sections of the train into the space. Of course, they missed many times, hitting the wall behind the couch, but that just made the game more challenging. After a while, Dad came to check on them and, to his horror, discovered they had put holes in the wall in several places. He was furious. After apologizing profusely to his sister and assuring her he would patch the wall, he took the boys home, telling them they would be punished. After some discussion, he and his wife told the boys there would be no TV for a whole month. The boys cried bitterly at first, but after a couple of days, they didn't seem to mind so much about the loss of TV time. Dad felt these boys were not learning a good enough lesson, and he asked me to come up with a better punishment.

"Do you think your boys knew that their game would damage the wall?" was my first question. He admitted that they probably didn't. I agreed with him that they had probably not intended to do wrong, so the best way to teach them not to do that again would be for them to make amends by helping their Dad to fix the wall.

He looked at me in disbelief and said, "You mean, let them help me apply putty to the wall? They would probably love to do that." I explained to him that true discipline is not about suffering, but about making amends and putting things right. He would be teaching them that when a wall is damaged, it takes a lot of time to repair, and maybe they would think about the consequences of their actions before they played their game next time. Taking away their TV time wasn't teaching them how to make a better choice next time, since it wasn't related to their actions. Dad bought a couple of small putty knives and his boys had not only a lesson in discipline but also on how to fix drywall.

It's Not A Plot To Drive You Crazy

66 Time Out

Time out is a method used by many parents to remove and isolate a child who is causing trouble. Often the child is sent to his room or to a safe location removed from everyone else. A period of time is allocated for the time out, sometimes by using one minute for each year of the child's age. A five year old, for example, would be given a 5 minute time out. However, many parents tell me that they've tried time out, but it doesn't work for them. Their expectations that the child would spend some time thinking about what he'd done wrong are rarely met. I believe time out doesn't work because it punishes but doesn't teach.

I sometimes ask parents to imagine that they are extremely agitated or angry. Then I ask them what they would do to calm down or cool off. Their responses include going for a walk, going to the gym to work out, talking to a friend to vent, removing themselves from the situation, taking deep breaths, and pounding a pillow. These are all healthy ways to cool down. Next, I ask them to imagine being back in that frustrated state again, except that this time their partner enters the room and says, "Boy, are you furious! You'd better sit on that chair over there. Now let's see, how old are you, thirty-five years old?"

Toolbox Skill

Show your children how you "cool down" when you feel out of control. Help your children to "cool down" on the rare occasions they display out-of-control behaviour.

"Okay. I'll set the timer for 35 minutes, and when the buzzer goes, you can leave the chair." Before I get to the end of this scenario, people begin to laugh because they realize how ridiculous it is. Next, I ask them to imagine how they might feel while sitting in the chair for the required 35 minutes. Most say they would be furious, and many say they would not stay in the chair. Not one ever said they might sit and think about what they did wrong! So why do we think children would be any different? We all need to calm down occasionally, but time out is probably not the best way to do it, for adults or for children. However, we can show our children how to calm down by using what I call the "cool down" process ourselves. If we feel as though we are close to losing control of our actions or words, it's best to remove ourselves from the situation and have some quiet time or a change of pace to calm ourselves down.

When we feel we are becoming overly frustrated with our children, then we need to "cool down" rather than "blow up." We can say, "I am feeling very angry, so I need to be by myself for a few moments." Then head for the bedroom, bathroom, or some place where you can be alone, even if only for a short time. Parents of young children usually stare at me in disbelief when I mention removing themselves rather than the children. So I add, "Yes, I know the children will follow you, weeping and wailing and pounding on the door." They are relieved to know that this happens to others, too! However, the most important part is that you, the parent, take a few moments to be alone, breathe deeply, imagine yourself in a relaxing place, and regain your composure. Parents hold the key to household harmony. If parents fall apart, the children usually follow suit, and then chaos reigns. Being away from the situation for a few seconds can help a parent to refocus and, by our example, children are learning a healthy way to deal with frustration.

Use a "cool down" for a child only on the rare occasions when he is displaying totally out-of-control behaviour that you must stop – hitting, biting, or any kind of abusive physical or emotional behaviour. Always remove the child, rather than scold him in front of others. Calmly but firmly let the child know, "It's not okay to hurt other people, so come and sit with me for a little while to calm down." The cooling down time isn't a punishment but an opportunity for the child to regain control of his behaviour.

If you have to impose a "cool down," keep the child with you. When a small child's emotions are out of alignment, it can feel quite terrifying to them. Children may not show it, but they do need the security of the parent's presence. If they want hugs or need to sit on your lap, it is a sign that they are regaining control. The hug is not a reward for the behaviour, however. To make this clear, you could say, "I think you are feeling sad that you hurt David. I'm glad you are calm again. Let me know when you are ready to go back and play." When we isolate a child by sending him to his bedroom,

It's Not A Plot To Drive You Crazy

we just increase his sense of insecurity. The bedroom can become a bad place to be, and may be the reason that a child who wakes up in the night doesn't want to stay in his room.

If children throw a tantrum as a result of being removed from a situation, it is their way of expressing frustration. As long as they are not hurting themselves or hurting property, just let them work it out and stay close by. It's virtually impossible to prevent a tantrum. If they are a physical danger to themselves or others, you may need to hold them snugly in your arms, or on your lap, until you feel the tension decrease. Flailing arms and legs can hurt, so it sometimes helps to hold the child facing outwards to avoid bruises.

During a "cool down," if they are sitting calmly and pick up a book or toy to play with, remember that the objective has been achieved and they are back in control. Avoid slipping into punishment mode and saying something like, "I hope you are thinking about what you've done." They are not, nor would we if we were in their shoes.

Many parents ask me if the situation should be discussed with the child after the child has calmed down. There is no right or wrong answer, because the parents are the best experts to evaluate their children's needs. Some children know they have crossed the line and do not need further explanation. Others may need or want to talk about it at a quieter time, or when the parent and child are feeling especially connected, such as bedtime.

As the child is cooling down, it's wise not to remind them again about their misbehaviour. Quite often, with the idea fresh in their minds again, they repeat what they did the first time. Simply say, "It's good to see you are ready to play again."

For children under two, "cool down" is seldom necessary or helpful. These little ones are not developmentally capable of grasping the concept. Removing them, followed by distraction or redirection works best for this age group. These children are exploring their environment without the knowledge of appropriate limits. Our job is to provide a safe environment so they can expand their boundaries and make their discoveries as safely as possible.

There's no set time for a "cool down." We cannot switch our emotions on and off according to a buzzer and neither can children. If we role model "cool down" times and teach our children to use them, we are arming them with a safe method of withdrawing from future difficult situations.

67 Using Choices

How can we teach our children to think for themselves and become accountable for the decisions they make in life? We begin by helping our young children make simple choices, and as they get older we gradually increase the number and scope of their choices until they are finally able to make all of them by themselves. When they've learned from a very early age to live with the choices they make, they'll be more likely to trust their judgment when it comes to the bigger life decisions, too.

Toolbox Skill

Choices teach children autonomy and the basics of decision-making. Knowing the difference between flexible and limited choices helps parents use this tool effectively.

Whenever I ask a group of parents if they use choices as part of their parenting strategy, they almost unanimously state that they do. My next question is, "Does giving choices always work with your children?" To this, the reply invariably is, "No, it only works sometimes, and we don't know what to do when the child throws in another option or refuses to choose." Of course, parents can't give choices all day long, but allowing choices can be a useful tool to help children begin to learn the process of making wise decisions. These are some of the first steps towards responsibility and independence.

Parents are often confused about using choices as a tool because choices fall into two types – flexible and limited. They are not always clear about when to use which type. A flexible choice allows a child to assert her individuality. She can choose from a broad selection of items. Flexible choices are usually easier for parents to offer because they are likely to be happy with whatever the child chooses. Letting the child pick which bedtime story to read, or select which toys to take to the beach are examples of flexible choices. A parent, however, offers limited choices when he presents two or three alternatives from which the child must choose. Limited choices require more careful guidance by the parent. When using choices, either flexible or limited, parents need to keep in mind that it is always their job to set the agenda.

A parent could offer a flexible choice when a child is getting dressed in the morning.

Parent: "Time to get dressed. We need to choose a shirt. How about either your red one or the blue striped one?"
Child: "I want to wear the green shirt that Grandma gave me."

It's not so much about how flexible the choice is, but how flexible the parent is with whatever the child suggests. Now, it so happens that the green shirt is clean and available. So my question to parents is, "Is it all right to allow the child to wear the green shirt? That wasn't one of the choices offered." Most parents feel that this is a "win-win" situation: the parent is pleased that the child is getting dressed and the child is thrilled to have some control and to wear what he wants. The result is harmony all round. You can't give choices all day long, but a few flexible choices allow the child some say in the daily routine.

Limited choices are useful when the adult needs to guide the child's decision about what is appropriate and what is not. Developmentally, the child may not yet possess the ability to make a wise choice. Allowing a young child to choose which clothes she wears to a family wedding could pose a problem because she may not understand the concept of appropriate attire for special functions. In this case, parents need to limit the selection, only allowing a choice of two or three outfits that would all be acceptable.

Let's look at another limited choice involving what to have for snack.

Parent: "For your snack today, would you like apple or cheese and crackers?"
Child: "I don't like that yucky stuff. I want candy for snack."

In this case, the child has little understanding about nutritional value, but she does know candy tastes pretty yummy! Some limits have to be in place here, and this is often where parents run into difficulty. It is so tempting to disagree and say, "No, candy is not a healthy snack." Do we honestly think we can convince a small child that candy is less desirable than fruit or cheese? Maybe the rare child will be convinced, but realistically, most know that candy tastes great and that's what they want. Who can blame a child for arguing and trying to get his way when sometimes he's allowed to throw in another option? After all, he's wearing the green shirt…. A limited choice can lead to an argument if it's not handled carefully.

Rather than being hooked into an argument, the parent can calmly repeat the choice, omitting any mention of the candy. "Apple, or cheese and crackers? Those are your choices." It is helpful if the parent then walks away, or turns away, so that her body language conveys the message to the child that she will not engage in an argument. Most children do not give up easily, and will follow the parent from room to room, whining about the candy they now desperately want. The parent could now suggest, "It looks like you are having a hard time deciding. Shall I choose for you?" At this point, some children try emotional blackmail, "If I can't have candy, I won't have anything," which in fact is a viable option, and theirs to choose. Eventually, the child will realize that he can make a choice, but only between the two things offered. It helps if the parent stays calm, and sticks with the offered choices. All this decision-making does take time, and requires firm resolve.

When your time is limited, here is a quick tip that often works for these more difficult, limited choices. It still remains important to ignore the child's option if it's not an appropriate choice. Repeat the original two choices, providing one more opportunity for the child to make a choice. If no decision is forthcoming, calmly say, "Oh, I see it's too hard for you to decide today. So I'll choose for you, and I pick cheese and crackers." At this point, I ask parents what they think the child will want now, and they all laugh and say, "Apple." Since the parent was initially happy with either choice, it's important for the parent to be flexible again. The child has now made a choice from the two options the parent offered and has taken another step on the path to learning to make his own decisions.

Limited choices also include the times when a child makes a choice without realizing that he has done so. Let's use bath time as an example. The child is having fun in the tub, but the water is cooling off. The child does not mind the cool water, and is not mature enough to realize it would be wise to get out.

Parent: "The water is cold now. So, in a few moments I'm going to hold out your towel, and that means it's time to get out."
Parent (later, while holding out the towel): "It's time to get out of the cold water now. Do you want to climb out on your own, or shall I help you?"

Even if the child resists getting out, she's made a choice. By the process of elimination, she's chosen to be helped. As you lift the angry child out of the tub, you could say, "I see you've chosen to let me help you get out. Perhaps tomorrow you'll get out on your own."

We are responsible for children's safety and well-being, so there will be many times when we have to help resistant children into car seats, insist on teeth being brushed, or take them home from the park when they don't want to leave. Many parents, understandably, find it difficult to make children do something they don't want to do. Using limited choices can help parents to give children a small share in the responsibility for some of the tough decisions we often have to make.

68 Consequences

Consequences teach cause and effect, and are a reminder that things go more smoothly when we are self-disciplined and make wise choices. Some consequences follow naturally from our behaviour, and some are imposed by others. The natural consequence of carelessly picking up broken glass may be a cut finger. The logical consequence of being late for work too many times is that we may be fired. Learning from the consequences of our actions is a lifelong process that begins in childhood.

Natural consequences are determined by the laws of nature, and are not set by the parent. Going outside in winter without mittens will result in cold hands. Touching a prickly cactus will cause pain. Nature is the parent's ally with these consequences. Of course, there are situations where it's not in the child's best interest to be allowed to learn from a natural consequence. We wouldn't let a child run out into the street to learn that the likely consequence is being hit by a car.

Toolbox Skill

Apply logical consequences when necessary. Consequences work best when they are appropriate to the situation, respectful of the child, and applied without anger soon after the event.

Sometimes parents need to create the logical consequences for their children's actions or behaviours when there is no immediate, obvious, natural consequence. Children need to experience the results of their actions to help them to learn to become accountable. Logical consequences need to be appropriate to the situation, applied as soon as possible, and be respectful of and understood by the child.

Here are some examples of appropriate logical consequences for three different age groups:

Action: A toddler pours juice on the floor.
Logical consequence: The toddler will clean up the spill, and may need help from the parent.

Action: A school-age child is consistently not ready for school on time.
Logical consequence: She must set her alarm for an earlier time in the morning, or go to bed earlier.

Action: A teenager has not done his required chores.
Logical consequence: He must delay going out with his friends until he completes the chores.

If the logical consequence does not have the result you want, you may need to extend the consequence. If the toddler continues to spill juice, then he'll need to continue to clean it up, or use a spill-proof cup for a while, returning to a normal cup again after a few days. If the school-age child continues to get up too late, she will need to keep adjusting the alarm time, or you could impose an even earlier bedtime until an improvement occurs. Anticipate that the child will protest. Ignore the protests, and remind the child that it is up to her to change the situation whenever she is ready. If the teen is still not getting his chores done, add an extra chore to his list, reminding him that chores come before pleasure. You could also request a written or verbal agreement from him that states when he'll do the extra chores.

Children are usually aware when they have pushed the limits too far. They may not like consequences, but they will accept them more readily if they feel fairly treated. But danger lurks in the parent's response to the misbehaviour. We have a tendency to lecture or berate our children when our anger flares. When a situation requires a consequence, it is important for us to remain calm. If we feel angry, we might need a "cool down" before deciding on a consequence, otherwise clear thinking becomes cloudy thinking. Faced with a calm, firm, and respectful adult, most children will realize and accept that it is their responsibility to make amends.

When you need to apply logical consequences, these suggestions may be useful:

- Always let children know they will be given another opportunity to try again. Consequences result from mistakes or errors in judgment. This is how the child learns a better way to do things next time.

- Small children may need an offer of assistance or cooperation from you when a consequence is imposed. But be careful that you don't do all the work!

- Avoid saying, "I told you so," however tempting it may be. That phrase is very discouraging for the child.

- If the misdemeanor is repeated, it may be necessary to adjust or lengthen the time of the consequence.

Parents often ask, "What do I do when I can't think of an appropriate consequence?" and "What do I do when my child refuses to follow through with the consequence?" These are both common challenges as children try to test the limits and the firmness of their parent's resolve.

If we are angry, it's often difficult to find a suitable consequence. In the heat of the moment, logic and reason can disappear. This is a time when an angry parent might mistakenly resort to using punishment to cause suffering, rather than teaching with discipline. Instead, try using one of the following ideas:

- Buy a little time to cool off, and let the child know what you are doing by saying, "This is serious. I need a little time to think about what needs to happen now." Consequences should be applied soon after the event, but a few minutes away from the situation can result in a more appropriate, logical consequence.

- Phone a friend whose parenting skills you trust, and ask him or her to suggest an appropriate consequence. Often another adult who is not directly involved in the situation can be more objective.

- Ask the child to think of a consequence. Curiously, children can be very hard on themselves and will often come up with severe consequences such as no TV for six months, or bread and water for life! Often the consequences they suggest are so bizarre that the parent is amused and jolted out of annoyance. Typically, then, the parent's solution is far less severe, and the child is grateful for such benevolence!

When a child refuses to follow through with a consequence and you feel that it is a battle worth pursuing, the most effective method seems to be to wait it out. Remain calm and determined in your approach. Until the child has made the appropriate amends, nothing else is going to happen. She won't be able to play, visit her friends, watch TV, or make phone calls. Life will become pretty boring until the consequence is taken care of. There may even be a tantrum as a result, but once it is over, ask her if she's now ready to do what needs to be done. In other words, you and your consequence won't go away. You can offer a little cooperation or assistance with the consequence, especially with very young children. If you have to go out, the consequence can wait until you return.

Logical consequences that teach accountability are an excellent way for a child to develop self-discipline. The child will learn more from a logical consequence than from a punishment.

69 Family Rules

Family rules need to be put in place as soon as children have an adequate level of understanding. These are basic rules that the whole family agrees are important and that must never be broken. It is important not to have too many rules. Two or three are plenty. They need to be posted in a place where the whole family can view them, perhaps on the fridge door. Family rules will differ from one family to the next, depending on what is important to each family, and the rules will change slightly as the children grow older. Decide together what the consequence will be if a rule is broken. Adults are not exempt!

Toolbox Skill

Discuss and implement family rules. They will do some of your work for you.

Here are a few examples of rules that might be appropriate for most families:

For toddlers and preschoolers:
- We are always kind and gentle.
- Running feet belong outside.

For school-age children:
- Ask before you borrow.
- Bathroom talk belongs in the bathroom.

For teens:
- We don't swear.
- Phone calls are limited to 15 minutes when anyone else needs the phone.

Don't worry about little ones not being able to read. Once the family members have discussed their rules and have written them out, the children will know what the rules are, and will impress their friends with their ability to "read" them.

There are some real bonuses to family rules. They can travel with us wherever we go. They can set limits for your children's interactions with siblings. The written word carries more weight than the little brother's words, and the parent doesn't have to get involved.

I have to admit that once our children were teenagers, they felt they needed some leeway with the family rule that "We don't swear." They assured us that there are times when one just has to swear, because nothing else will do. They told us that when you bump your head or pinch your finger in a drawer, an expletive just happens. Family rules change as children get older, and it's important to allow the rules to grow as the children do.

70 Take Time to Smell the Roses

When we add the responsibilities of parenting to our already busy lives, we may forget to take the time to enjoy the journey with our children and to smell the roses along the way. Rather than noticing and celebrating our children's progress, we often spend much of our energy reacting to their negative behaviours. Our children are constantly showing us that they are slowly, but surely, advancing towards independence. If we don't watch for them, we may miss the signs of maturity that they are trying to show us.

While he was at preschool there were some concerns about our older son's ability to concentrate. After fretting and worrying for some time, we finally realized this was the same child who could spend hours watching an ant going about its daily business. He was showing us in his own way that he

Toolbox Skill

Take time to smell the roses. Enjoy the parenting journey with your children. In countless ways, they are showing you what an excellent job you're doing.

did have the ability to concentrate for long periods of time. It just wasn't in school.

So often I've heard parents comment in utter exasperation, "I don't understand it. My son can name every player in the hockey league, but he constantly forgets to bring his homework home." Or I'll hear parents complain about how disorganized a child is, while overlooking the fact that this same child can coordinate a whole team of friends to play together at the local park. Sometimes we are so focused on the big picture, worrying about how our children will master all the skills necessary to become responsible adults, that we may forget to celebrate the small, important steps they are making each day towards that goal.

As children mature, they are immersed in daily, exciting discoveries about their world. If we allow them to, they can also lead us back to the excitement of discovery, reminding us to enjoy life along the way.

Having a clear parenting plan and a toolbox full of practical skills will enable you to parent with confidence and enjoyment. Encourage your parenting efforts by noticing and complimenting yourself on the areas in which you excel. Maybe you have endless patience, are a good listener, or make play times together lots of fun. Our good qualities are gifts that we share with our children.

When you feel confused or puzzled by a child's behaviour, it helps to take a look at what is happening through the eyes of the child. If you understand the child's point of view it can help you select an appropriate tool for the situation. Your favourite tools are already working well for you and as you parent, you'll add new and useful tools. As well, your inner resources of common sense and gut instinct will always be there to guide you.

It's not a plot to drive you crazy. It's an exciting journey of discovery both for parents and children. So with your toolbox at your side, have fun and enjoy the ride.